Wake Me When You Leave

About the Author

Elisa Donovan, known as an actress for her roles in *Clueless*, *Beverly Hills 90210*, and *Sabrina, the Teenage Witch*, graduated from Eugene Lang College at The New School University in NYC, where she studied dramatic literature, acting, and writing. She has been a celebrity mom blogger for people.com and is the narrator of the bestsellers *Lean In* and *Option B*. The film version of *Wake Me When You Leave* is in development and will be her directorial debut. Elisa lives in San Francisco with her husband and daughter.

ELISA DONOVAN

Wake Me When You Leave

Love and Encouragement via
Dreams from the Other Side

Llewellyn Publications
Woodbury, Minnesota

FIRST EDITION
First Printing, 2021

Book design by Samantha Peterson
Cover design by Kevin R. Brown
Photos provided by the author

Llewellyn Publications is a registered trademark of Llewellyn Worldwide Ltd.

Library of Congress Cataloging-in-Publication Data
Names: Donovan, Elisa, author.
Title: Wake me when you leave : love and encouragement via dreams from the other side / Elisa Donovan.
Description: First edition. | Woodbury, Minnesota : Llewellyn Publications, 2021. | Includes bibliographical references. | Summary: "After prominent roles in Clueless and Beverly Hills 90210, Elisa Donovan's career was on the fast track. Until her show is unexpectedly cancelled, her relationship ends, and her father is diagnosed with terminal cancer. This book chronicles Elisa's journey out of despair and heartbreak, with nudges from a subtle spiritual presence that could only be her father looking out for her. By sharing the lessons and challenges that the universe sent to her, Elisa inspires those who are learning to let go after a loss so they can live again with authenticity, hope, and humor"—Provided by publisher.
Identifiers: LCCN 2021005094 (print) | LCCN 2021005095 (ebook) | ISBN 9780738768205 (paperback) | ISBN 9780738768380 (ebook)
Subjects: LCSH: Grief. | Fathers—Death. | Donovan, Elisa, 1979—Family. | Spirits.
Classification: LCC BF575.G7 D667 2021 (print) | LCC BF575.G7 (ebook) | DDC 155.9/37—dc23
LC record available at https://lccn.loc.gov/2021005094
LC ebook record available at https://lccn.loc.gov/2021005095

Llewellyn Publications
A Division of Llewellyn Worldwide Ltd.
2143 Wooddale Drive
Woodbury, MN 55125-2989
www.llewellyn.com

Printed in the United States of America

*The wound is the place where
the Light enters you.*
—Rumi

For Dad,
Sweet dreams.

Contents

Preface

"I'm scared, Dad," I said, as the storm escalated and bellowed around us.

"There's nothing to be scared of, kiddo," he replied, his words like a magic salve, abating my fears.

I was seven years old and the Yankees had just won. It was a hot summer night, and we exited the stadium surrounded by the camaraderie of thousands of victorious New Yorkers. We piled in the car to go home, me sandwiched in between my brother and sister in the back. I leaned over the front seat between Mom and Dad and looked out the windshield, exhilarated by the throngs of people on the streets at ten o'clock at night. Horns beeped, Latin music pulsed out car windows, people yelled to one another. I was convinced I could sit right there and watch it all go on forever. But I was asleep in the backseat before we even got out of the Bronx.

Somewhere on the Long Island Expressway, I was awakened by the sound of rain. By the time we reached our driveway back in Northport, it was pouring. Dad jumped out to open the garage door, holding his coat over his head to block the rain. He jumped back in the driver's seat nearly drenched and pulled the car inside.

Twenty minutes later I was lying in bed staring at the ceiling, petrified of the mounting storm. The summer air was balmy and warm, but it felt like the whole world had just gotten cold. The thunder and lightning came in angry bolts, doors slammed shut, and it scared the life out of me. I leapt out of bed and ran down the hall and down the stairs.

Louis Armstrong was crooning "When You're Smiling" quietly on the stereo as Dad sat outside on the screened-in porch on one of the white PVC patio chairs with plastic cushions that left crisscrossed marks on your skin when you sat on them. He had a tumbler in his hand, half-filled with what looked like ice water but could've been a gin and tonic. He was reading a book—maybe Tom Clancy, but probably Robert Ludlum—utterly unperturbed by the storm swirling around him.

Suddenly I felt extra special to be up so late while my older siblings were already in bed asleep. I was dressed in my favorite summer sleeping uniform: blue terrycloth shorts and an oversized white cotton V-neck undershirt of my father's, in tatters from hundreds of washes and soft as anything I'd ever felt. I gripped the shag rug beneath my feet between my toes. From my perch at the edge of the living room, barely peeking my head out past the sliding glass door, I whispered, "Daddy?"

He looked up from his book. "Hey, kiddo, what are you doing up?"

"The storm. I can't sleep."

"Come here, sit down." He motioned for me to come out. Although I was terrified at the prospect of going any closer to the tempest, his calm amidst the raging rain made me venture out onto the porch in my bare feet. I walked over to him tentatively.

I wanted to sit on his lap, but I didn't know if I should. So I sat in the chair next to him, the cool ribbed plastic of the cushion sticking to the backs of my legs.

"I'm scared, Daddy," I said. He looked out at the mounting weather beyond the screens, and then he reached over and patted my knee.

"There's nothing to be scared of, kiddo," he said. "It's just rain, and a lot of noise and … nature." We sat there together and listened to the thunder launch out of the darkness unprovoked. We watched the lightning ignite the sky; and his steady presence, his indifferent fearlessness, made me feel safe. I began to focus on the sound of the water pelting the roof, and the sound became like a rhythmic song. I felt the warmth of the summer rain and could smell the sweetness of it. I waited for the rumble of thunder to come again, and it came like a kettledrum, and I waited with anticipation for the flash of lightning to return and illuminate us and our whole backyard like a grand stage. With a crackle and an explosion of light, the storm reached its crescendo and then slowly began to subside. And as the rain eventually lessened to a light drizzle, and the thunder and lightning retreated back to their corners somewhere far away in heaven, my fears turned to wonder and love.

"Are you okay now?" he asked. I looked up at him with such pure belief and faith like he was a sorcerer. He was magic.

"Yeah. Thanks, Daddy."

The glimmering stars peeked through the blackness. The stillness of the fresh night air surrounded us. Feeling more confident, I moved over and sat on his lap and he wrapped me up in a hug. I didn't want the moment to end.

With his arms around me, he patted his hand on my chest. "I love you, kiddo. Go to sleep now."

I stalled for a few seconds, enveloped in his hug, savoring the feeling of safety. Then I moved down from his lap to go. As I reached the threshold of the porch, I turned back and looked at him. His gaze remained on the distant sky, absentmindedly humming along to Louis, smiling along with the whole world. I watched him, wide-eyed and biting my lip, awed by his simple strength.

I ran back upstairs filled with a calm and comforted glee that my dad had shared a secret with me, and I knew I was safe to go to sleep that night. I crawled into bed, pulling the covers up to my neck, and I prayed for another thunderstorm to come again soon.

Introduction

My father and I did not have a storybook kind of relationship. In fact, we were somewhat of a mystery to one another. He was the definitive patriarch who created stability for our family, and I looked up to him with equal parts adoration and aggravation. In large part my dad struggled to understand me and my choices, and I constantly challenged his. Then over a very short period of time I lost my job and my relationship, and my father was diagnosed with cancer and died. In what felt like an instant, I was stripped of literally everything that gave me a sense of safety, joy, purpose, and accomplishment. I was rattled and rudderless. But a funny thing happens when you don't have anything left to hold on to: you let go.

In my grief, I began to connect to my father through a series of visitations, dreams, and odd occurrences.

I had always been fascinated with dreams. Sometime around the age of eight, I had a recurring dream with a giant spider. The spider would appear in different places—through the sliding glass door of our screened-in porch, its talon-like legs itching to crack the door open and creep in to grab me; outside my bedroom in the hallway, desperate to enter as I ran to slam the door on it. I would wake up crying and my mom would come in and hold me. "It was just a bad dream," she would say. It didn't occur to either of us to investigate the dreams, to dive into them instead of retreating and shutting them out. It wasn't until years later that I read about the symbolic meaning of spiders, and it's pretty powerful: Yes, they can symbolize fears and anxieties, but they're also about creativity. The spider in its web is the symbol of the center of the world, "everything converging to a central point; the ceaseless building and destroying (weaving and killing) symbolizes the ceaseless alternation of forces on which the stability of the Universe depends."* Yowza. Pretty lofty stuff for an eight-year-old to metabolize, sure. But what if I had acknowledged the dream rather than stifling it? What if I moved toward it instead of retreating in fear? Might I have discovered something awesome? There is such rich material in our dreams. They are chomping at the bit to give us information and help us listen to our inner knowledge.

I've also been known to sleepwalk. Once when I was eleven, I got up in the middle of the night to take a shower. In my pajamas. I turned on all the lights in the hallway and my bedroom and the bathroom, getting ready for my day. My mother came into the bathroom squinty-eyed and aghast, asking me what I was doing. I informed her I was "getting ready for school, obviously." When I was fourteen, I had a sleepover with my friend Gina. I got up in the middle of the night and walked over to the window, opened it, and shouted, "I think they're here. It's time to get up. Come on, get up!" More recently my husband, and many of our closest

---

* Juan Eduardo Cirlot, *A Dictionary of Symbols*, trans. by Jack Sage, 2nd edition (Mineola, NY: Dover 2002), n.p.

friends, will recall the time I sleepwalked naked outside of the Four Seasons in Santa Barbara at a friends' wedding. It felt cold out there at 2:30 a.m. so I started banging on our villa door, livid with my husband for making me go outside on whatever errand I believed I was tasked to do. "Charlie! It's too cold out here for this. Let me in!"

I have always been interested in the messages of our dreams and our subconscious, as well as in the afterlife and past lives, psychics, and spirituality. I was born on the same day as my grandmother, a woman who was an avid visitor to psychics and read her own tarot cards. But grief can do some tricky things to our perceptions. So when I started to connect more deeply to these things as my dad got sick and passed, I at times felt like I was descending into a kind of madness.

This period of time seemed to encompass all things and their opposing forces: heartbreak and humor, despair and hope, dark and light, clumsiness and grace, and so on. It began a transformational journey for me that I didn't know I needed to have. I learned that sometimes you must lose everything in order to find your way. This book is my journey of falling apart and putting myself back together. It is my personal hero's journey, my Personal Legend.

This book is about how ultimately hopeful life is—that even when someone we love dies, they never really leave us. Even after someone dies, it is never too late to make peace. *Wake Me When You Leave* is my discovery of love, loss, and priorities. It juxtaposes the realities of my real life against the backdrop of Hollywood and the facade of an actor's life. I hope it ripples through the hearts of everyone who reads it. My intent is to inspire authenticity and hope. And to make you laugh your tail off through your tears.

This has been a long journey. One I am still walking. My grand hope is that this book helps you to keep walking yours with grace and awe and laughter. Trust you're being looked after, because you are.

chapter
ONE

It was the summer of 2003 and I was sitting in my car in the parking lot of the Mayfair Market eating a bag of Veggie Booty when my older brother called to tell me our dad had cancer.

"Dad has terminal cancer of the esophagus with an inoperable tumor," Drew barked at me like it was my fault, like along with all of my other colossal screwups, now I had the audacity to give our dad a terminal illness. I immediately thought of how they always said the word in movies: "*cancer...*" in a whisper; as though it was a dirty word, or a delicacy. Coming out of my brother's mouth it sounded like a chainsaw or a pipe bomb, but nothing resembling a whisper.

I knew I was supposed to say something, that I should respond to Drew, but I couldn't. It felt like the ground had fallen out from beneath me, and if I looked down I wouldn't see the floor mats of my car but my feet dangling in the air, suspended like I was sitting on a Ferris wheel ride. I was staring straight ahead through the LA-smog-induced grime that coated the front windshield of my car. It was July and like a thousand degrees outside, and there was this burly husky sitting on the pavement staring right back at me. He was tied to a bike rack at the entrance to the market, wearily panting in the dead summer heat. The drool dripped out of his mouth and he looked back at me exhaustedly like, Yup, that's what he said. CANCER.

"What?" I said finally, like I didn't hear Drew the first time, forcing him to repeat it; making me hear it twice.

"Cancer of the esophagus with an inoperable tumor," he snapped. "Soooo, yeah. The doctor says he should start chemo, like, yesterday. And that, basically, is the crux of the biscuit."

My brother is always saying things like "the crux of the biscuit." He mixes metaphors with a great sense of humor, which a shrink might say masks his inability to be intimate, but we won't go there because neither will he. Drew is gay and somewhat reserved, unless he's very hammered or very angry, which used to happen more often than one might consider … ideal. He lived on the same property with my parents, a strong contributing factor to both his hammered and angry spells. He sounded relatively calm at the moment. But I imagined plans to become the former were brewing, which would eventually morph him into the latter, and he would sound like a drunken and belligerent Johnny Weir by sundown.

"Mom is an absolute basket case," he continued, sounding a little bit like I was somehow responsible for *that* too. I imagined my mom in the doctor's office: rummaging through her enormous purse in search of a pen or tissues or her lipstick. She was probably making a list of some kind to distract herself. She's big on lists. They give her a feeling of organization and litter her kitchen counter like index card confetti. She was probably fumbling around with a little pad and paper, avoiding eye contact, talking a lot but not listening, trying to maintain her bright smile and positive outlook. She must be a wreck. And driving my dad insane.

Drew went on and I couldn't understand what he was saying, couldn't metabolize it. I just kept thinking, Do people really *get* cancer? Isn't cancer just some illusive terminology for a faux disease that's used to scare people into quitting smoking and eating more fiber? I mean, *my dad* doesn't get cancer. He's never even sick. He's invincible.

"Helloo? Wheezer? Are you still there?" My family has called me Wheezer since I was a kid, after the character on *The Little Rascals*—the one who sucked his thumb, carried a blanket around, and never spoke. Never has a person grown up to defy their childhood nickname more than me.

"Yes, yes. I'm here," I said. "How long does he have?"

"They don't know exactly. Maybe a few months."

This was like reading hieroglyphics to me, like he was speaking in tongues or something. I mean, chemo? A few months? The doctors must have been wrong. They said things like "months to live" on soap operas but not in real life. This was insanity. Did he mean Dad wouldn't even be here for Thanksgiving? What about Christmas?

"Oh, crap. Here comes Mom."

Then I heard a fumbling with the phone and a muffled laugh and my mother's jovial, upbeat voice. "HEY WHEEZE! HOW ARE YA?" she said, sounding puzzlingly elated. Like she was at a class reunion or a toddler's birthday party.

"Hi, Mom."

"So LISTEN, we were just—listen—" she was laughing so hard, she had trouble getting the words out, "HAVE YOU SEEN *FINDING NEMO*?"

I mean, WTF.

My mother, Charlotte, speaks in capital letters. She's the kind of woman who has a full face of makeup on and her hair done in her sleep. You could surprise her and knock on her front door at one in the morning on a random Tuesday, and she would answer bright-eyed with frosty lipstick and a blowout.

"You know, that movie?"

"Yes, Mom. I've seen *Finding Nemo.*"

"WELL. We just thought that we'd bring home some fun movies to watch! You know, to cheer up your father! Just in case he wants to see something funny!" I imagined her offering him an ice cream cone or a lollipop, telling him she'd take him on a pony ride when he got better.

"How big is the tumor, Mom?"

"Oh! Well, the TUMOR is about the size of a—what'd the doctor say, Drew?" She paused. Drew started a response in the background, and then she cut him off and drove on with excitement, "A GOLF BALL! Well, bigger than a golf ball, more like a lemon! Or maybe not that big, maybe more like a lime. Oh yes, that's it! I think we decided on a LIME!" Her voice was energetic and manic, and she sounded genuinely pleased that she remembered which kind of fruit the growth resembled. Should there be any future dispute, she had her facts straight: this tumor was no grapefruit, it was still hovering around the size of things that garnish cocktails.

I tried to decipher some truthful data. "Has the cancer spread?"

"OH well, YES! It has spread." Then her voice became hushed but still exuberant, like she just realized this party was supposed to be a surprise. "In fact, it has gone to his LYMPH NODES. Well, now that is ... WELL, IT'S PRETTY—NOT SO GOOD." I heard her voice crack, and the opening inhale of a sob.

I think she dropped the phone, and the next voice I heard was my brother's. "Okay, she's losing it. But she's the one who knew what he had before the doctors did." Drew went on to tell me that Mom had done her own "research" on the internet. And before they went in for the results she deduced that Dad had cancer of the esophagus, which was exactly what the doctor wound up telling them. "Maybe she's a genius."

"Yeah, maybe she is. Where's Rita?" I asked, referring to our oldest sister who has a general aversion to our family that keeps her at bay from anything resembling an ability to communicate with us. Rita wears ill-fitting mismatched sweatsuits and has had the same pair of sneakers since 1985. It's safe to say that Rita is on her own program. She prefers animals to people. She's a dog groomer. She and Dad have always had a bond of sorts. They are remarkably different in nearly every discernible way, save two: their shared tendency toward crankiness and irritability where the rest of us are concerned, and a similarity in the physicality of their faces that is uncanny. Sometimes they would sit in the living room propped up in front of the television in nearly identical chairs, and I would see their profiles and the way they both nodded off to sleep watching some rerun of *Friends*, and I'd have to do a double take they looked so much alike.

"She's inside with Dad—Oh wait, here they are," he said.

I heard my mom stifle a pained yelp and begin a high-pitched holler. "JACK! RITA! Come on, we're going home to watch *FINDING NEMO!*"

"Great idea, Mom. That's a kids movie. And the mother dies!" I could practically see Rita's curmudgeon-in-training expression through the phone, huffing and puffing till she blew the whole hospital down. Rita vacillates between silence and explosive rage in these kinds of situations. I imagined her hovering over my dad like a homing pigeon. He was probably so pissed.

"Jesus, you'd think I lost a limb or something. Christ—I'm not crippled, Rita." Bingo. "Drew, who are you talking to? Charlotte, come on, get in the car."

"Jack, do you really think you should drive?"

"Yeah Dad, you shouldn't *drive*!"

"What are they doing?" I said, trying to insert myself.

"They're arguing about who's going to drive," Drew answered.

"Is that Elisa? Give me the phone." Dad cleared his throat as he picked up. "Hey honey, how's it going there? Are you at work? They shouldn't have bothered you at work."

"No, I—I finished early today," I lied. "Dad, how are you doing?"

"Me? I'm fine. I'm fine! Everybody's acting like I'm going to keel over right here in the parking lot, but I'm fine. Charlotte, please get in the car." He took a long exhale, then said to me, "It's like herding cats, you may recall, sweetheart."

"Dad, I'm going to see when I can get home—"

"What? Jesus, don't come home. Honey, don't be silly. Don't come home. There's nothing for you to do." I thought I would feel more relieved to be let off the hook, but I didn't. I just felt nauseous. "Rita? Thank you, but I can sit down on my own. *Please* get in the car. Charlotte. You are *not* driving. Let's go."

"Jack, you are in no condition—"

"Too many lefts turns back to the house, Charlotte. Get *in*!" I heard my mom mumbling something about her "blind spot" and how "we always get there just the same …!" Dad reiterated, "You know your mother and her refusal to make left turns. Just getting out of this parking lot could take an hour."

"Dad! You shouldn't be driving!" Rita sounded like she was actually frothing at the mouth. I heard the car door slam, drowning out Rita. "Okay, we have to go to Home Depot. We'll catch up with you later. I love you, sweetheart." And he was gone. Then Drew came back.

"So. So yeah."

"...Home Depot?"

"Yup. That seems to be the priority."

"Umm. Okay." There was a pause on the line. I knew what was hanging in the air, but I held my breath hoping to avoid the question. No such luck.

"I don't know what your plans are—" Drew started, but I cut him off before he could ask.

"Well, I can't come home right now. I have to see about work, you know see if I can ..."

"Yeah, okay. Let us know."

"All right."

We hung up.

I zoned out staring at the bag of Veggie Booty and the residue of its green powder still stuck to my fingertips. Dad always called Veggie Booty "dirt in a bag." How could I eat Veggie Booty if Dad was dying? Suddenly it seemed grossly inappropriate, like there had to be certain things you don't *do* as soon as you have a father with cancer. Fun and simple things that you lose the luxury of indulging in. I was sure that eating snack foods straight out of the bag in your car had to be one of those things.

I looked at the groceries sitting next to me, a pint of mango sorbet melted through the paper bag, forming a small puddle on the script from my now-defunct television show that lay beneath it.

Oh God. And there's that.

From the moment Drew dropped the bomb about Dad's cancer, I had completely forgotten about the other phone call I had received updating me on the status of my life. But now it came back to me with a sickly clarity.

"You got the boot. *Sabrina*'s cancelled," my agent, Jerry, said curtly through the phone, like he *wasn't* telling me I was suddenly unemployed, like I *didn't* already have a lifestyle I could barely afford. I heard him guzzling something followed by a guttural hacking sound emanating from the bowels of his gut. "Jesus, this cleanse. I feel like somebody put a freaking Brillo pad in my intestines." Jerry hadn't slept since the late '90s. He was the kind of guy who had books like *Kabbalah, Healthy Living, and Longevity for Dummies* on his desk, with a *Playboy* and an open bag of Taco Bell perched on top of it. He was never doing less than four things at one time: he could be brokering a deal for a client on the nth installment of some mediocre franchise and scheduling a dental appointment for his mother, all while he was waist-deep bidding on a boat on eBay.

"Wait—what—?" I started.

"That's it. They're probably replacing you guys with a sitcom starring that Southern comedian who just got out of rehab. Can't wait to see *that* debris littering the airwaves this fall," he said, loving his own wit. "Whatever. It's great news. That show was a piece of crap anyway."

"What? I don't think—"

"You were the best thing on it. I gotta run." And with a "Good God, who can digest this garbage?" he hung up.

I watched the moisture from the sorbet seep onto the now curled-up edges of the script, threatening to devour it whole and leave it to drown in a puddle of its own swill, much like the flawless Shakespearean tragicomedy that my life seemed to be unfolding into with wicked speed. I wanted to call someone. And then I suddenly thought I should probably stay off of the phone altogether, since it seemed to be a portal to everything dark and dying.

I watched the heat from the LA sun rising off of the asphalt outside my window. I sat there in my car, keys in the ignition, engine off, windows sealed shut. It was so silent. People walked by outside my window, continuing on with their lives. In slow motion they entered and exited the market, with bags and cell phones and shopping carts and children. Beyond the cocoon of my car, a horn sounded somewhere. There was so much activity out there, but I was utterly still. And I sat there like that for a very long time.

Eventually I started the car and pulled out onto Franklin Avenue into late afternoon traffic. I made a left onto Gower out of habit, forcing me to pass Paramount Studios, where I would no longer be going every morning at the crack of dawn. Six years of five a.m. calls and fourteen-hour days culminating in a pool of disappointment on the passenger's seat next to me. I continued down Gower until it dead-ended at Melrose. Paramount sat like an old flame with unfinished business flanking my left, steadfast and threatening. I made the melancholy turn away from her and headed toward home.

I pulled into the garage below my building. New construction condos, a hybrid of NYC old-school cool and Los Angeles clean-lined modernity. I parked and grabbed the soggy grocery bag from the front seat. I prayed there wouldn't be anyone on the elevator. What would I say to them? I felt comatose and out of touch and yet simultaneously like it might be a great time to strike up a conversation. As I walked out of the empty elevator, I began really wondering what I was supposed to do. I so desperately wanted to be told what to do.

I exited on the third floor into the atrium of the building. The idyllic sound of the fountain in the center flowing like a waterfall, mixed with the melody of "Egg," the only hopeful and optimistic song that my musician boyfriend, Cooper, had ever recorded. I opened the front door to my apartment to find Cooper on the couch, sitting unusually close to some girl I didn't recognize, who swayed along to the music. The girl looked elfin and tortured, like a cross between something out of a *Lord of the Rings* movie and a Marilyn Manson video. The buoyant lyrics about time finally revealing that we are all "just fine" dominated the room like an ironic taunt. Cooper looked creepily predatory and guilty as all get-out and greeted me with a tentative, "Well, howdy."

Something about this girl's vibe made me to want to swaddle her in something warm and cozy, while something else told me I might like to run her over with my car.

"My dad has cancer," I blurted, standing in the foyer with the nearly broken, soggy bag hanging limply in my hand. "Oh. And I'm unemployed." I put the bag down and walked into the bathroom. I looked in the mirror and searched for some sign of change. Some physical mark. Like I'd see a cross on my forehead, branded by cancer and failure.

When I came out, the gloomy Frodo-loving handmaiden was gone, and Cooper walked over to me.

"I'm sorry, Red," he whispered, pulling me into a hug. I didn't cry, I just hung stiffly in his arms. I didn't really know what I was feeling. I was numb. Over his shoulder I could see a photo of my dad and me in a swimming pool when I was two. He held me in his arms while I floated; we both had huge smiles on our faces. Mine was impish and goofy, biting my bottom lip; his was proud and entertained, like I'd just done something mischievous and brilliant and he couldn't help but laugh. I thought of his sense of humor and the way his singular laugh could erupt out of him when you least expected it, when you weren't sure if he was going to ground you or hug you. How I'd push the boundaries of his patience to the limit, always hoping it would be the hug. How I'd call him in a crisis and immediately be put at ease just by hearing his "Hey, kiddo" on the other end of the phone. Now I tried to remember the last real conversation we had, and I drew a blank.

"I need to take a nap," I said, sliding away from Cooper. I walked back into the bedroom and slipped under the covers. My body was absorbed into the mattress and I prayed that when I woke up things would be different. That somehow my life would go back to what it was an hour ago. How could things go so monstrously awry in so brief a span of time? Still engulfed by this overwhelming sensation that I should be doing something, that time was ticking away, I did the logical thing: I escaped into a glutinous sleep.

I am sitting in a hotel restaurant with a lot of men when my teeth start falling out in shards and slivers, flowing in an unending stream out of my mouth. I futilely attempt to catch the pieces in my hands but there are just so many of them. And each time I touch my mouth another shred of tooth falls. I excuse myself to go get another napkin, leaving the heap of slivered teeth on the table. When I return, I see the waiter has removed my pile of teeth and I ask him where they went. He is disgusted and tells me so, like I was purposely pulling some prank to humiliate him. As though I would *choose* to have a mouthful of gums? I begin to argue with him that I literally need the teeth so that I can bring them to my dentist who will decipher the shards, get to the root of the problem, and tell me why they are falling out. Then the dentist will put them back in my mouth, I am certain of it. Suddenly my brother is here, and I explain my dilemma to him. He tells me to stop exaggerating, to stop being so dramatic. Then I hold up my bag of teeth and give him a full all-gum smile.

I was awakened by the violent ring of my cell. Jerry again. I was hesitant to pick up, but then I figured it wasn't like there could be any *more* bad news.

"Hey, Jerry."

"It's not going any further on that pilot. Sorry, hon." *Jeez, this phone!*

"What? Why? I thought after the work session—"

"The network has a hard-on for this chick that's in the new Apatow movie."

"But she's, like, seventeen—"

"They're going to age it down a little."

"But she's supposed to have a teenaged son!"

"Look, everyone is an asshole! On to the next!" he boomed. He sounded so callous and casual about my life falling apart. *I have got to be imagining this.* "Speaking of—that talk show isn't going to work out either. The studio decided they don't want an actress on the panel. You're not relatable to moms in Ohio." *I'm definitely putting this phone in the microwave on HIGH.*

"What? But they sent me a pair of Jimmy Choos and a gift basket!"

"Hey, I'm sure you can keep the shoes. Don't sweat it. Why don't you go get a massage or something? Go take a spin class. I gotta take this." Click.

I peeled myself off the bed and slugged my way into the living room to lie down on top of Cooper, who was nearly catatonic on the couch. After an Olympic-size pause, he said, "So that girl … That was Maizey." Aaaaaand that explained my vehicular woman-slaughter fantasies. The tortured elfin creature who made a stealthy exit earlier was his ex-girlfriend. He had always described Maizey as more like his kid than his girlfriend, so when she disappeared and moved in with some old guy in Orange County I thought there was nothing else to say about her. *Until today.* For such a wayward and wounded little thing, her timing really was impeccable.

"You have got to be kidding me." I sat up.

"She's like a broken bird," Cooper explained.

"You said you two never should have been together in the first place!"

"I think we should probably take a step back." *Wait a minute— could he actually be breaking up with me right now?* "I need to go back and fit that all together. Make it fit. I never got to do that with Maizey, so it's always dangling out there with no way to file it. It's that filing cabinet part of my brain. It's how my mind works, like the article said," he offered, referring to a test he recently aced in *Newsweek* entitled, "If You Answer Yes to These 30 Questions You Have Asperger's."

In that moment if I had the balls and the biceps to do it, I would've picked up Cooper and all of his "behavioral insensitivity to other people's feelings" (question #4) and tossed him out my living room window. But I didn't. I was dumbfounded and I started scream-crying instead. This had zero impact. (See question #5: "appears to lack empathy.")

"You know we both got into this like a train wreck, Red. It isn't working," he said matter-of-factly.

"You cannot be doing this right now. You just can't. It's—it's mean!" I was unraveling and it was very messy and there wasn't a thing I could do about it.

"What about what *you* did to Martin?" he asked pragmatically. And just like that, with laser precision he stunned the tiny unspoken raging corner of my heart that I thought I kept so craftily hidden. It sucked the air right out of me. "Come on Red, we were both racing against our pasts here. I know you still think about him."

Since the mere idea of adding *my* ex into that day seemed like too sick of a development even for the wickedest of temperaments, I used my wily powers of elucidation and quickly formed a defense.

"That is totally irrelevant! Martin and I weren't meant to be! Don't you see how it's all supposed to work out?" I blurted, gesticulating wildly. "You and me—WE are supposed to be together!"

"Come here," Cooper opened his arms to me, like I should bring it in for a "bro" hug. When I didn't move to him, he moved to me. "Bye, Red," he whispered with a hearty pat on my back.

"You can't go," I begged. "You just can't…"

But apparently, he could.

As the door closed behind him, I slid down the wall onto the floor and stared at the back of the door for a while. Eventually I shifted my gaze over to the grain in the wood floor and started to wonder if this was all a test, some confounding secret game of endurance. In this escalating shit-fest that was my life, if I could withstand enough, did I get a prize? Enlightenment? Eternal peace? A freaking chocolate bar?

chapter
TWO

If I told you my dad wasn't around a lot when I was a kid, it would be both accurate and misleading.

I was born in Upstate New York in Poughkeepsie, but my dad was transferred to New York City when I was six. He said he didn't want us growing up in the "City" (with a capital C) because it was too dirty and overcrowded and dangerous, so we moved to the suburbs of Long Island. But while Northport was a somewhat idyllic little town with a quaint Main Street and fresh lobster available on the daily, it also turned out to be the site of a Satanic ritualistic killing by several teenagers high on angel dust. Seriously. You can Google that. I remember finding this out through the grapevine in gym class one day. I went home to my dad and said, "I haven't heard of this kind of thing happening in the 'City.'" He was not amused.

For most of my elementary school and early teen years, my dad left the house at five a.m. to beat the commuting traffic, and he didn't get back home until after seven-thirty at night. Now that I have a daughter of my own, I marvel at my mom's ability to stay upright parenting three kids essentially solo all week. Dad also traveled pretty often for work, which meant sometimes he was completely gone for a week at a time, so on many nights we were a foursome instead of a pentagon. We developed our own dynamic that took specific advantage of Dad's absence. I recall my Mom chasing Drew around the entire house on more than one occasion, wielding some large object and trying to swat him with it as he cackled and eluded her swing.

Rita was the one closest to my dad in a unique way, so she may have felt his absence more profoundly than Drew and I did. Even though she is seven years older than me and two years older than Drew, she was never a typical eldest sibling. She never tried to rule the roost or tell us what to do. *We* were the ones who terrorized *her*. She was always trying to escape our antics; she just wanted to be left alone to draw or read.

When Drew and I weren't trying to scare Rita or make her participate in a blanket-fort obstacle course, we were making movies in the basement, putting on magic shows, or setting up makeshift rope swings on trees in the yard. I looked up to Drew and would do anything he told me to do. He used to sell me "treasures" from his closet. Like dried out Magic Markers and empty rolls of Scotch tape. I remember telling my mom I desperately needed two dollars one rainy afternoon and when she asked to know for what exactly, I revealed a torn piece of loose-leaf paper and a broken crayon. Drew was also obsessed with Barbra Streisand. (Anyone who was surprised when my brother came out as gay years later really just hadn't been paying attention!) He had read somewhere that Barbra had a house out east near where we kept our horses. As soon as he got his driver's license, we drove to this random house in Nissequogue and Drew made me get out of the car holding up our boom box blasting "Memory." (Babs did not appear.)

Dad being away also meant that we went out to dinner. A lot. Because my mom in a kitchen is like an owl at a disco: just picturing it is nearly impossible. Charlotte was never a fan of cooking. Or cleaning, or sewing, or feeding things if we're going to get right down to it. A lost button on a shirt was always cause for alarm and confusion in our house. For years I thought ferns were meant to be brown and crusty; I thought they were *supposed* to die every few weeks and then you just bought a new one. As a kid, I thought the oven was a storage space. I only learned it was a space for cooking things when I went to a friend's house and saw her mother take something hot out of the oven and said, "Oh, that's what you guys use that for? We put Cheez Doodles and Tupperware in there."

But even though my dad was often gone during the week, I always remember him being there with us on the weekends. I was a competitive gymnast from the age of seven until I was eleven, and both my parents drove to the ends of the earth for competitions that lasted all day. They were repaid for their efforts by my insistence that they leave the gymnasium when it was my turn to compete. I didn't want them to watch me; it made me nervous. Can you imagine? You give up your Saturday and drive all the way to Timbuktu to watch some other guy's kid do a back handspring. *Retroactive apology here, Mom and Dad.* And when I started to grow out of gymnastics (literally, I started to grow), I began riding horses competitively. Yet another entirely time- and finance-consuming endeavor (that my brother had been doing for years) that took the whole family up and down the East Coast every weekend from March through October.

We were lucky kids. We grew up in a stable and fortunate environment. My parents always supported us in anything we wanted to do if they could.

To a point.

All along I had also been taking acting lessons. Since I had played Ralph Rotten in the infamous Bellerose Avenue Elementary First Grade production of *Westward Ho! Ho! Ho!* (hold your applause, please), I was hooked. I had no idea at the time that you could make a career out of this, that some people actually got paid to become other people in front of other people. And although I was shy as a kid and didn't like a lot of attention focused on me, on stage I didn't mind it. It felt different. Once I reached junior high, I knew that acting was what I wanted to do with my life and nothing was going to stand in my way of it. Even my father.

Of course, junior high also coincides with that magical time when one believes that not only does one's fourteen-year-old self know absolutely everything, but one's parents know exactly zero about anything at all. My swift rebellion came in the form of a full and obliterating pursuit of art and acting, as well as the choice to become a vegan after watching one of those PETA videos where they poke a bunny in the eye with a lipstick. I went so far as to march down Fifth Avenue in Manhattan carrying a "FUR IS MURDER" sign. Being a staunch carnivore and having just bought my mom a mink coat, my dad couldn't conceive of why I would ever do such a ludicrous thing, and who was teaching me this garbage anyway?

This "new me" was made complete by the required nonconformist artist uniform: combat boots and crinolines, black everything. While my dad was stupefied by my appearance, my mom tried to negotiate, and we made a deal: I would have designated "father clothes," e.g., "We are going to the Johnsons' for dinner tonight. Put on your father clothes." This meant nothing torn, spiked, black, or scratchy and see-through. No T-shirts as skirts, no underwear as outerwear.

There was an additional factor worth mentioning that contributed to my complete commitment to my true artist self: in the middle of eighth grade, all of my girlfriends turned against me. In an afternoon, I went from being a popular, well-adjusted kid to a zero. I remember it seemed to coincide with a popular boy that I liked liking me more than one of these girls, and the next thing I knew no one would talk to me. Those girls were mean, and they enjoyed being mean, because fourteen-year-old kids can be especially cruel to one another and are adept at exposing and exploiting one another's vulnerabilities. It was devastating for me at the time, and I almost left school because of it. But I wound up becoming grateful for that experience because it showed me who I am and what I value. It steered me further toward creativity and kindness, and it allowed me to blossom as the true weirdo and slightly left-of-center human that I am proud to be. And as a result, I began to develop friendships with like-minded and like-hearted people. Friends that I made movies and music videos with on the weekends and created art installations and demonstrations with on our lunch hour at school.

I discovered *my people.*

And the major silver lining and best payback ever? Years later, I would base my character in *Clueless* on those eighth grade meanies. So, as they say, *The joke is on you, suckers!*

It turned out that father clothes were also appropriate for auditions. In eleventh grade I got my first manager from a theater showcase I had done with my acting coach. I would go to school in my nonconformist gear and then exit the bathroom after lunch like Clark Kent, unrecognizable in a crewneck sweater and khakis.

Mom would pick me up and we would take the train into the city to audition for tampon commercials and after-school specials.

When it came time to apply to college, I informed Dad that I wanted to take a year off and go to an acting studio full time. This was met by my father with the amount of enthusiasm of a salt lick in a desert. At the dinner table one night we negotiated an agreement: I could go to the Michael Chekhov Acting Studio full time for one year and then I would go to college.

I moved into the West Village of Manhattan that summer and put my nose to the grindstone. I went to the studio five days a week, worked at a restaurant, did theater, and slept very little. After six months of this, my father said we needed to have a conversation.

"You've been at this for six months and you're not famous yet, so I think it's time to get serious."

Wow.

That did not feel good to hear. I can still feel the flames igniting up the sides of my head and out the top of my cranium.

But his words didn't make me want to quit. Quite to the contrary, they made me even more determined than ever. I agreed I would go to college, but only so that I could become an educated actress. I applied to and was accepted at Eugene Lang College at The New School University in New York City and started that fall. I went to class five days a week and took additional acting classes outside of school in between. I waitressed and bartended at night and continued to go on audition after audition and not book one job. (FYI: This is what is diplomatically referred to as "resilience building." I like to call it "complete and total f*&%ing-s***-I-want-to-smash-my-head-against-a-brick-wall building." Actors get real familiar with this sensation.)

Officially being in college gave my dad some peace of mind, but we would still argue about politics and social conditions and he would tell me in no uncertain terms, "You don't know what you're talking about. Do you even know what 'gentrification' means? I don't know who these 'nonconformist artists' are but I don't see them paying your rent and your tuition." He would come to see me in plays and tell me how good I was, but he still didn't see how it all amounted to anything. My father just couldn't understand me and the desires of my life: to be an actress and make art and make a difference in the world in *my* way.

It's not that this surprised me. I mean, my dad was an altar boy growing up and became a traditional Republican. He liked salted peanuts and perfect Manhattans on the rocks. He liked to watch golf on TV, and he believed in fixing a thing if it broke rather than buying a new one. He was frugal but generous, very smart but not complicated. Everywhere he went he knew someone: airports, restaurants, shopping malls. Jack was the guy that made sure that no one in his family wanted for anything. As a teenager, he took care of his widowed mother and three siblings and then put himself through college to become an executive at AT&T. And he did it without announcement or fanfare. He just took care of it.

Then, when he retired early at the age of sixty-one from his high-stress corporate job in New York City, he moved my mom to central North Carolina, bought fifty-six acres of land and turned it into a horse farm for my brother. He built thousands of feet of post-and-board paddocks himself with a little tractor, an auger, and a hammer. He would be up at dawn helping my brother with the horses. He would drive all the way up to Long Island to pick up my sister when she came down for a visit. Why did he do this? Because Rita wouldn't fly and Jack didn't want her driving that far alone and, as previously mentioned, Rita is on her own program.

Jack was a good dad and people loved him.

People also love my mother, Charlotte. She was a beauty queen! At the age of twenty, she was Miss Buffalo and was awarded second runner-up in the Miss New York State pageant. And the only reason she didn't win the title was because when asked the infamous million-dollar question: "If you could have one wish, what would it be?" Instead of saying "world peace" or "to feed the starving," a beaming Charlotte Hino said, "TO WIN THIS CONTEST!"

I've always tried to explain the special nature of my mother to people who have never met her: eternally upbeat, violently optimistic, not fond of silences. I used to do elaborate impressions of her with direct quotes for my friends all of the time. Everyone found them entertaining but only those that had actually *met* her ever believed they were true.

My father, however, was not always as dazzled by Charlotte's charm. He would lose patience with her and become irritated with her flakiness. It was like my mom was paying some karmic debt she was unaware of, and my dad was supposed to be generally irate with her for the bulk of this lifetime so she would disregard her true feelings and needs in favor of a flightier balloon-like existence.

Once when I was in college, I asked my mother if she ever had dreams. Her first sparkly response was that she "slept like a log!" I clarified by saying I meant had she ever wanted to do anything else with her life, aside from being a stay-at-home mom. Then she answered so swiftly, it was as if she had been waiting her whole life to be asked that question.

"Oh, yes! I wanted to work! You know I was planning to open my own charm school and teach modeling!" I was dumbfounded. She had never mentioned any of this to me before. And what the heck was a charm school?

I asked her why she never pursued either of those things, and she said that my father told her she wasn't allowed to work. And then she was pregnant, and that's just what you did back then. *I mean, was that really what it was like? Weren't all of those house-wife commercials tongue-in-cheek?* But then I realized Dad proba-bly saw that as a badge of his success as a provider: his wife didn't have to work.

Then I asked her how that made her feel. Didn't it bother her to be forced to stay at home and have children with no choice in the matter?

"Oh yes, I was terribly depressed after I had each one of you," she said. Then after a pause, "Especially you."

Gulp. She went on, dropping one bomb after another. I asked her if she ever talked to anyone about all of this. And she said yes, she had gone to see a psychiatrist who told her to get over it and get it together.

"He told me that I had a family now and I had to be a mother." I imagined her spilling her guts about what surely was undiag-nosed postpartum depression to some conventional and cold old man, whose solution was to tell her to get her shit together. I couldn't fathom it.

Then with a gleeful and heartbreaking smile of denial, she said, "And so I did! I just got over it!"

In that moment I understood so much of her life. I thought about what it must have been like to have a full spirit and a lot of feelings and nowhere to put them. I also understood why I felt like such a freak my whole life, why all the years of tortured punk-rock-teen-angst that I had spent kicking and dying for understanding had been met by her with a perplexed expression of put-upon vacancy: for if she could make me believe that she was unconscious and uncomprehending, she would remain safe from having to answer to whatever might lie kicking and dying inside of her.

This also put into perspective why my move to Los Angeles had a different effect on each of my parents. With one semester left of college, I announced that I would be turning down a (paying) theater gig and a possible (very *big*) paying gig on a soap opera to move to Los Angeles and work with my affiliate agency out there. Charlotte's eyes lit up and she gasped with excitement at the doors of opportunity opening!

And Jack said point-blank, "No, you're not."

I moved to LA knowing two people: my agent (*not* Jerry) and my friend Jennifer, a playwright I had worked with several times in New York. Two weeks later, I booked an episode of the sitcom *Blossom*, and a month after that, I booked the film *Clueless*.

Dad was happy, if dubious, that at least I had a paycheck. When he could turn on the television and miraculously see me there, he slowly warmed to the idea that maybe, just maybe, I wasn't going to be a complete failure. But my dad was a concrete realist, a numbers guy. So it wasn't until I was able to start paying my own rent and buy a car that he started to see that maybe this acting thing had legs.

I remember the first time my parents came to visit me on set. I was shooting the TV series of *Clueless* on the Paramount lot. I was so excited for them to drive onto the lot through those iconic gates and see me hard at work, shooting a fourteen-hour day. I stepped out of hair and makeup to find Dad standing there holding Mom's purse like a briefcase.

"This is like watching the grass grow," he said. When I asked him where Mom was, he pointed to the wardrobe trailer. The door opened and Charlotte stepped down in a new outfit, waving wildly.

"THEY GAVE ME A PART!" she beamed, looking both totally surprised this was happening and utterly certain it was exactly what she expected to happen. Amy Heckerling was directing that episode, and she made Mom an extra on a park bench. And Mom couldn't have been happier about it. "Look, honey! It's *Forrest Gump*'s bench! RUN, FORREST, RUN!" Amy was so sweet with her. She had to do at least a dozen takes because Charlotte kept distracting from the actors in the scene. "Cut! Charlotte! Don't look into the lens!" and "Cut! Charlotte, you're a scene stealer! Just try to blend in!" It was amazing and I loved it. My mom framed her paycheck, and she still asks me where her residuals are.

My career continued on a nice trajectory. I was in a flow of working on a series for nine months out of the year, doing a film on my hiatus, then going back to work on the series. And when *Clueless* was cancelled after three seasons, I booked *Sabrina, the Teenage Witch* and started the same process again for three more years. I had a boyfriend I loved and a steady job I was passionate about. Things were good. And my underlying belief was always *And they are only going to get better.*

chapter
THREE

Dad started chemo almost immediately after his diagnosis, and I was paralyzed at the thought of going home and seeing him sick.

I was dreading it because I knew that, like any other uncomfortable or intimate challenge our family had ever encountered, we wouldn't talk about it directly. I hoped for some emergency to come up and prevent me from leaving. But then I thought, What exactly is a bigger emergency than my dad dying? I went to book a flight home, secretly hoping there wouldn't be anything available. But there was a nine a.m. the next day.

I deliberately waited to pack my bag until that morning, sluggishly walking from dresser to suitcase and back. I pondered toiletries, weighing which toothbrush to bring, which shampoo. What I was doing was ridiculous, but I didn't stop doing it. I was trying to miss my flight.

I arrived at the airport like a train wreck: sweatpants with holes in them, hair tied on top of my head, no makeup on, and bright white zit cream masking the doozie of a spot that had sprouted on my chin overnight. I breezed through security, my final hopes of missing the flight dashed, and headed to the gate. Grateful for a window seat, I curled myself up in it, knees tucked to my chest. Somewhere over Texas, I just started weeping. I guess I had been holding it in, and then the flood gates opened, and I couldn't stop. There was a nun sitting next to me, full habit on and a rosary around her neck. I thought of my Catholic upbringing. Baptism, confirmation, church every Sunday; I had gladly fulfilled the basic screening process required to get me into heaven, and I agreed with it all. Until my first year of college when my brother came out as gay. I couldn't reconcile that the church considered him a sinner just because he might love someone named, say, "Steve," so I deliberately lapsed. But now, all these years later, this kind-faced soul looked over at me with a teacherly expression—not exactly warm, but knowledgeable—and saw me crying, and I imagined us having an in-depth conversation about illness and family and loss. I could open up and ask all of the right questions, and she would put me at ease and give me all of the right answers. She'd tell me What Jesus Would Do. She'd give the entire plane a blessing and tell me my father will be fine!

"Don't cry, dear," the angel said. "It's okay."

I couldn't really speak. But I was so relieved that she might help me, that she seemed to be reading my mind, I tried to get words out. "It's … I can't. It's my—"

"Don't cry," she said again, patting my hand. "Planes take off and land all the time. It's perfectly safe."

"What? Oh, no it's not that—I'm not—" I stumbled.

"We'll be there in no time, dear," she said with that same knowing smile, very pleased with herself. "This is nothing. You'll see."

When I got off of the plane in Fayetteville, my parents were waiting at the gate. I got a glimpse of them through the throng of bodies in the tiny terminal before they saw me, and for that one suspended moment, I was free. *I can leave now before they see me. I can turn around and get back on the plane, safe up in the air from this reality.*

The first thing I noticed about my dad were his glasses. It was like they had gotten bigger, gigantic even; he was a cartoon Mr. Magoo. When I got closer to him, I realized it was because he had lost so much weight his whole body had shrunk and his eyes appeared enlarged. We said hello and gave awkward hugs. My mom had her typical big smile plastered on her face and she nervously hugged me, repeatedly patted me on the back and kissed my cheek. Dad extended an arm to bring me into his chest. I held him tight.

"Hi, kiddo. It's good to see you honey." He rubbed my head for a minute, and I was gutted. I had forgotten how much comfort this small gesture always gave me. We headed out to the car, hand in hand.

The ride to the house was uneasy and bleak despite my mom's attempts to stay one step ahead of the sadness with her continuous chatter. Her small talk efforts to alleviate the heaviness permeating the car did not make that elephant lounging in the back seat next to me disappear. His enormous wrinkly legs spread themselves along the seat, practically pushing me out the window, but I remained silent with my face pressed up against the glass, unwittingly endorsing the denial.

The countryside of North Carolina is verdant and lush in late summer. The greenery is abundant, rolling hills and Carolina red maples line the highway, their vibrant hues framing the horizon. On my parents' road the trees turned to huge longleaf pines, and their daunting and shadowy presence engulfed the entrance to their property. An expansive field of jumps and paddocks made up the right side, and the pine trees and American elms enveloped the left. The house and barn they built for Drew and his horses were at the far end straight ahead. My parents' house was to the left with a circular drive in front, a modest five-bedroom ranch.

A gaggle of dogs came bounding out of the house as we pulled up, including my ninety-five-pound Rhodesian Ridgeback, Zulie. Working the crazy hours that I did and never being home, I had sent Zulie to live with my parents a couple of years prior. Seeing her running around the farm like that with the other dogs always reassured me that I had made the right decision.

Since I hadn't grown up in that house, I didn't have any room that was really mine. My sister would call me Goldilocks when I came at Christmastime, because I would switch bedrooms nightly until I found the one that felt just right. That trip, I picked the room off of the kitchen for its own private bath and easy escape route to outside. Although my parents didn't know it, I had recently started smoking again (the perfect appendage for the daughter of a cancer victim) and I wanted to be able to indulge secretly and freely. Right on schedule my regression set in, and within seconds I was back in junior high on Long Island smoking cigarettes out the bathroom window with the shower running.

Since my mom had never met a moment that didn't deserve photographic documentation, there were framed images from virtually every episode in our lives covering every flat surface of the house. Horse shows, birthdays, family trips, graduations, holidays, and trips to the supermarket on any given Wednesday. I zeroed in on a photo of me as Amber from the movie *Clueless* in a ridiculous over-the-top fur jacket and leather pants. I had enormous Audrey Hepburn sunglasses on and a giant purse I could barely keep on my shoulder. I looked at that picture and at once couldn't remember the exact moment it was taken, yet fiercely wished I was back in it. Back to someone fussing with my hair, telling me where to stand, top-sticking my bra to my shirt to keep it in place. I wanted to escape into the fantasy of hitting my mark and saying the lines of some other person in some fictionalized situation. Then I thought, Why the hell does she still have these photos out? Everyone in our family knew I had been severely anorexic when we shot that movie, that I had gone into the freaking hospital in the middle of it. Those pictures were twisted reminders of how colossally ill I had become and how no one seemed to think there was anything wrong with that. The pictures also perfectly exemplified my family's commitment to denial and how proudly they clung to it.

Suddenly I wanted to set my hair on fire and run screaming from the room.

Instead, I stuffed myself into the familiar wetsuit of smiles and silence reserved specifically for visits with the parents. But as skintight and asphyxiating as that suit was, it still couldn't keep the ocean of waves from crashing down on all of us.

———

So after my smoking shower and an uncomfortable dinner, Dad sat at the table with Zulie at his feet while Mom fluttered like a hummingbird, busying herself cleaning countertops. I reentered from the bathroom and wanted to jump up and down screaming, "How can this be happening? What are we going to do? You are dying and I'm scared shitless and I don't know what to say!" But

I didn't. I just stood there impotent and silent. Seeing me, Mom broke the silence.

"Hey, honey! We're just deciding if Dad wants some ice cream!" she said, like it *wasn't* totally preposterous that she had to help Dad make a decision about a bowl of ice cream. "I know you won't go near it, sweetheart, but we have some chocolate chip mint that's DELISH!"

Dad sat at the table looking inconclusive. I went over and sat down with him and struggled to find the words. My dad was a proud man and I could see him trying to navigate his noticeable weakness. In the past he would've been on the couch with his bowl of ice cream half finished already, either ignoring us all or yelling to me to come in and finish *The Times* crossword with him. But now here he was at the kitchen table awaiting my mom's lead, subdued and uncertain.

"Is there any of that Neapolitan?" he blurted, suddenly struck with the idea. That made me laugh out loud. Who called ice cream by that antiquated name anymore? I mean, who does that? I thought of my brother and sister and me as kids, fighting over the chocolate and vanilla, the unluckiest sucker always left with the strawberry. My dad would have a fit about the unequal consumption of the three flavors; it would irritate him to no end (the waste and the injustice!). His wife eating only the vanilla and his sneaky children scooping out every last edge of the chocolate when he wasn't looking, leaving him to discover the strawberry, despondent and alone in the corner of the carton.

"So … are you feeling okay?" I started. "With the chemo?" I had been there for almost twenty-four hours and there had been no direct mention of why I was there in the first place. I was grasping for some sort of acknowledgment of his illness.

"Oh yeah, it hasn't been too bad," he said quickly. Then after a slight pause, "Not yet anyway." He stared a moment, and then he didn't want the ice cream anymore. "I think I'll go to bed. I'm pretty beat." He got up like molasses, kissed me on the top of the head, and walked out of the kitchen. I looked up at my mom for a response. She was still wiping down the counter, the rag nearly disintegrated. Then she looked up at me with a smile. "Are you sure you don't want any chocolate chip mint? IT REALLY IS GOOD!"

I stared her down. My eyes were ablaze, brimming with tears, and I could think of nothing but smoking.

"I'm going for a walk," I said.

I was barely out the front door when I lit up. I sucked it down and waited for the nicotine to hit and give me a temporary kick. All I really wanted to do was call my ex-boyfriend Martin. I still couldn't shake the sickly sensation that I had made a terrible mistake by breaking up with him.

Maybe Martin and I can get back together, I romanticized. *Maybe he'll forgive me for giving up too soon. Maybe I was being petulant, I can be so fickle… Maybe he will hear my voice and we will magically return to when we first met!* As I hit Martin's number on speed dial, I realized that phone calls made in a frenzied emotional panic are much like drunk dialing: Never a good idea. Always done with great fervor and bold certainty that what you are doing is right, yet with utter disregard for the current reality of your life.

Martin was the reason I had originally quit smoking in the first place. So I tried to silence my exhales as I dialed, not wanting him to know that I'd returned to it. I was inhaling the cigarette as fast as the phone was ringing, getting in as many drags as I could before he picked up. Every pause between rings was cavernous, full of endless possibility and the threat of sheer disappointment.

Martin picked up with a tentative and questioning, "Hi."

Okay, hold it. Backstory. Martin and me. It's necessary. Bear with me.

It's October of 2001 and Martin and I kiss for the first time at six in the morning after an all-night wrap party, post shooting an eighteen-hour day on an MTV special in Las Vegas. I'm not at my best: caked-on makeup, pasty-faced and dry-eyed outside of the Hard Rock Hotel under the halogen lights and bright crackling beams of morning sun. If a kiss can overcome those elements, it's a kiss to be reckoned with.

I fly straight back to work for the table read of that week's episode of *Sabrina*. On zero sleep and adrenaline, I am glowing. A week later we have dinner, and I know we're going to be together.

By Thanksgiving we're in Hawaii together, and he gets food poisoning. I bring back Pedialyte and popsicles from the Haleiwa grocery store. I put cool towels on his head, and for the first time in my life, I want to be a wife and a mother and a part of a union.

We're at Melissa's New Year's Eve masquerade ball, dancing until the wee hours and drinking some good luck black-eyed pea soup, when he takes my face in his hands in front of the fireplace and tells me he loves me for the first time. I can't get the smell of his neck and the way we kiss out of my mind.

I break my wrist doing back handsprings in the wet grass on the Fourth of July and he takes care of me. He shaves my legs for me in the tub, which isn't nearly as sexy as it sounds because he has to shave my armpits too. He drives back early from surfing in Mexico with the boys to go and buy a Christmas tree with me. We lie on the cool sand of Bluebird Beach in Laguna, my face nuzzled in his sweatshirt. We're singing karaoke in Rosarito. We're tandem surfing in Waikiki. We're cliff diving in Maui. We're in NYC on Halloween: a fallen angel in red pleather and Winnie-the-Pooh with a cigar. We're laughing until daybreak.

Then one day he stands in my living room and says he never wants to get married; he doesn't believe in it. "But neither do you, right?" he says. And I fall to pieces, because I had only just realized that I actually was the kind of girl that wanted to get married and have a gaggle of uber-cool kids. Ironically, because he made me feel like that kind of girl. I start to feel like my depth is destroying parts of him, slowly dampening his charmed life. I'm tarnishing Peter Pan. And then after almost two years together, we break up in the middle of the night. He stays through the night because neither of us can fathom the separation. We sleep entwined and make the bed together the next morning. I weep as he weeps and packs up his stuff. All that crap he had—his surfboards, his toys. His shirts on dry cleaning hangers, his CDs, his sneakers. The Frank Lloyd Wright cement slab I painted for him for Christmas, the one I thought would be the front stoop of our first house together.

I watch him drive away, his Volvo wagon packed to the gills. I watch him become a tiny black speck as he disappears in the distance. My heart shatters and the fragments splinter into a multitude of indeterminable parts. I wonder how I will function; I wonder how I will ever get out of bed again.

A week later, desperate and seeking a savior, I rebound into Cooper.

> A week after that Martin reaches out to talk; he misses me.
> Then he finds out about Cooper and he is crushed.
> And I am crushed.
> And then my dad gets cancer.

"Hi." His voice. It had only been a few weeks since I'd heard it but God, how I missed it.

"Hey," I said. The words wouldn't really come. I wanted him to read my mind and scoop me up and save me. But he waited for me to start. "I just wanted to talk to you. The thing is, I'm in North Carolina at my parents' house. It's my dad. He has cancer." I felt his heart open and sink to the ground.

"Oh, Elisa. I'm so sorry," he said. "Where is it? What kind?" We continued with the specifics and he asked me all of the right questions. His mom had been a registered nurse for many years and had beaten her own cervical cancer, not to mention his father who had beaten prostate cancer years ago. I wanted this connection with someone who knew something about what we were going through; someone I had a true history with. Someone who knew my dad.

My dad loved Martin. Martin was bright and shiny and happy and relatively stable. The deal was sealed when we had come to visit last spring.

In the center of the circular driveway in front of my parents' house there was a bird feeder. Renegade flying squirrels would constantly invade the bird feeder and eat the seeds my mother put in it for the birds. Charlotte would spy the squirrels from the kitchen window as they descended on the feeder and in a humorously irate tirade, she would run out and kick the bird feeder, scaring the life out of the squirrels and sending them soaring. As soon as Dad watched Martin run outside and perform the same ritual on behalf of Mom, kicking the wooden pole with the enthusiasm of a madman, he was considered a keeper.

"How is your mom holding up?" Martin asked.

"Well, she's cleaning up and vacuuming through it."

"Right." I could hear the slightest smile in his voice, he knew Charlotte. But then the distance came back and he tried to wrap it up. "I'm really sorry to hear this. So. I hope everything turns out okay."

I wanted to leap through the phone and throw myself into his lap in Laguna Beach. Go swimming in the ocean with him.

"Send my good wishes to both of your parents," he said.

Please, please don't hang up!

He waited for me to say goodbye. I wouldn't. A monumental pause that encompassed all things big and small transpired. Still, I couldn't bring myself to speak.

"I'm going to hang up now, okay Elisa? I'm really sorry about your dad." Suddenly desperation overtook me.

"Wait, Martin—I just..." The tears rolled down my cheeks and into my mouth. The cigarette had burnt down to a nub, searing my fingertips. "I'm sorry, I just, I miss you. And I wanted to talk to you."

"Where's Cooper?" he asked, getting to the point; instantaneously bursting my balloon of hope with one strategic pinprick.

"LA." I felt the breeze from the door closing right in my face.

"I have to go. Please send my best to your dad, okay?"

"No, wait—"

"Goodbye." He hung up.

"Okay," I said into the phone, even though he was already gone. "Okay. I'm okay. It's okay." I repeated "okay" into the empty phone line, trying to convince myself that it was the truth.

The perversity of my situation felt like a revenge of the very circumstances I had created. I looked up to see the bird feeder standing directly in front of me, inanimate and lifeless in the night air. I didn't kick it.

———————

The following morning my parents drove me to the airport and the silence was so torturous it tore through my eardrums like a butcher knife. We arrived curbside and, sleep deprived and near tears, I leapt out of the car to grab my suitcase before my dad could get to it. I was scared that he wouldn't be able to lift it, and I couldn't bear the thought of seeing him attempt to and fail.

Charlotte took out her camera to capture our morbid parting so that one day that moment, too, would hang on the wall next to maybe a white-water rafting trip and she could say, "Oh, this one is from when Dad was so sick with the CHEMO! Remember?"

"Mom. Seriously?" I asked, looking at my father's gaunt appearance. His sunken grey skin and Iris Apfel–looking glasses staring back at me.

"Yes, come on now!" she said, ushering us together and aiming the lens. "SMILE!" And with one click, she immortalized that moment I was fiercely hoping I could just forget.

chapter
FOUR

The following Monday, my best friend Ruth called and told me her father—who used to bring us egg sandwiches on Saturday mornings after sleepovers when we were in high school, and through a sick twist of fate had *also* been sick with cancer—died that morning. If you had told me at the age of fifteen when Ruth and I met that we would become the best of friends and that one day our fathers would be dying of cancer at the very same time, I would have said that not only are you fatalistic but please save the hyperbole for the books and movies. On that Monday morning, the irony of our reality was almost too potent to acknowledge. Our history was so deep and our bond of friendship so strong, we barely needed to speak. She knew I would be there for her.

So I got back on a plane the next morning and flew back to the East Coast to Long Island for the funeral. It wasn't lost on me that going to be there for Ruth's dad was infinitely easier for me than going home to see my own family. That was the kind of transference of emotional support I was able to pull off in that moment. Somehow it allowed me to rationalize having left my own parents; I was going to give support where it would actually be received.

Even though I was back in my hometown where I grew up, I felt displaced when I arrived. Normally I stayed with Ruth at her dad's apartment when I came for a visit; we would bunk together like siblings. But they had actual family there then for the services and there was no space for the surrogate. I drove around in a rented SUV that felt and looked like a milk truck. I searched for the comfort of remembrance in that place, the informality and simplicity, hoping to be engulfed in the safety of my youth. I drove by the house I grew up in and slowed down in front. Like a stalker I peeked through the forest of trees and landscaping out front and could just catch a glimpse of the fence in the backyard. Whoever owned it now let the rose bushes my father had planted die.

I drove across town, past the train station and my high school and headed to Ruth's. I pulled up in front of her little green duplex with the cement front stoop, the spot where we used to smoke cigarettes after school while her dad was at work. I headed inside and up the steep flight of stairs.

Ruth was sitting alone in the tiny kitchen with a stack of photo albums in front of her on the table. She had a mass of thick, black hair and a round face that was usually plastered with a mischievous and amused grin. Ruth had a witty and devious sense of humor, with an enormous presence that could light up a room. But sitting at the table right then, she appeared deflated and small. She turned to me. We locked eyes and I felt a rush of something that I couldn't quite explain. At once it was an understanding, a knowingness, a relief, a peace, a pain, a screaming. We simultaneously said, "Hi, Mona," our childhood nickname for one another, born so long ago we couldn't remember where it began. But it was *us*.

"Let's go for a drive," I said. She smiled, almost relief on her face. She grabbed her purse and a to-go iced tea (Ruth never got in a car without a beverage) and we headed outside.

Seeing my absurd vehicle fit for a family of eight, she said, "What the F, Mona? Do you have an entourage with you these days?"

"Yeah, and we're delivering milk," I said. "I feel like I'm in a freakin' dairy truck." And for the first time in what felt like ages, I exhaled.

I started the car and headed toward Ocean Avenue, made a right. At the bottom of the hill on either corner sat St. Phillips Church and that other Episcopalian church nobody ever went to, except once in high school for our friend Shawn's funeral. *Was that the last time someone I know died?* I wondered. We made the right onto Main Street and a warm wave of familiarity came over me. I looked over to the passenger seat at Ruth and saw the same face that walked with me down the middle of this same street fifteen years earlier, both of us too young to even drive. Skipping on a warm summer night, out past our curfews. Lying to our parents so we could be one with the night and outlast the moon, solving the operatic problems of our newly teenaged lives.

Now here we were adults, with the weight of experience inside us both, but relishing the moment: the simple pleasure of a drive, a great song on the stereo, and an assurance of one another's company. Memories flooded me as we drove: summer sunburns, giggles in the dark, hikes through thorny trees and chaos, singing into hairbrushes, tears of heartache, cutting class and forging notes. Now, soon, I would hold her hand at the funeral of her father and she would most likely do the same for me. When, I wondered? How soon? Next year? Next month? Next week? While I was attuned to Ruth's grief, it struck me suddenly that this felt like a dry run for my own father's funeral. I was partly outside of myself watching, looking for clues as to how I would act, what I would do, what I would feel. I watched Ruth, hoping to find answers. *What do you look like when you've just lost your dad?*

We drove down past the movie theater and the ice cream parlor, past all of the restaurants and pubs to the end of the street and pulled into the parking lot of the harbor. That was our spot. I turned off the ignition and we looked out at the water. And for the first time ever, neither of us knew what to say.

———————

Over the next three days, throughout the wake and the funeral, I made my sole focus taking care of Ruth. I picked her up, drove her places, talked to her, left her alone, made sure she ate, let her have space, organized friends getting together, held her hand, and just got her whatever she needed. *I am so my father's daughter.* I wanted to fix things. I was aware of how much better it would make me feel if I could just take care of something for her. Problem solve. Normally Ruth was the mother hen, the alpha of our group of girlfriends. She always designated what we were doing and when and with whom, always driving. But right then she was adrift, and I just wanted her to know that I would catch her as best I could, point her in the direction she needed to be at any given time. I wanted her to know she could surrender.

What my fishbowl, myopically self-involved thinking neglected to see, however, is what *Ruth* might've wanted. Turned out, it *was not* all of that attention. All of the tending to her was giving her hives, making her feel like now she in turn had to help *me* manage all of *my* sudden responsibilities. Turned out I was super annoying and only marginally helpful. Basically, I was a pain in the ass.

This made me feel terrible. And then I realized, *Oh. All of this is actually what I would want.* Someone to just be there. Hover. To do what I couldn't do myself, to just let me go through it and be my witness, to let me remember, to let me forget, to know that it was going to get ugly and that would be okay, to let me know that nothing is too much. *That I am not too much.*

I was also aware of the ever-nagging sensation that I was avoiding my own reality. Caring for Ruth and grieving her dad had been grounding me somehow, keeping me in the present moment. But when I understood my presence wasn't as saintly and required as I created it to be in my grasping mind, and I realized that I needed to leave Ruth to grieve in her own way, I was lost. I knew she was grateful that I came, but I could no more save her from her grief than she could preempt my own. I realized this transference I'd attempted hadn't magically eradicated the very real facts of my own life, and that began my descent.

———

I got back to LA and I lay down on the floor of my living room. I didn't unpack my bag, it seemed futile. The phone rang.

"Hey, Mom."

"Hey, hon! I've got some news! Dad had his fourth chemo session today! Ugh, I'm telling you, he looks MORBID but they say it's helping!"

"… okay."

"Oh! And Tigger died!" she said brightly, sounding like she just remembered to tell me a friend stopped by. "Poor dog! Your brother is beside himself. I was home when she went. And you know how BIG she is! I had to drag her across the floor and out into the car." I couldn't bear to think of this. To picture my mom dragging that giant dead dog, with Dad bedridden and vomiting in their bedroom.

"Where was Drew? Why didn't he help you?" *God, he is such a baby! It's his freaking dog in the first place! Of course, he leaves it for Mom to handle. Oh, I could kill him!*

"He wasn't home. ANYHOO! Just wanted to catch you up. How was the funeral? I sent Ruth a note. That poor girl! Oh, it's just SO SAD," she said, like I *didn't* have a dad and she *didn't* have a husband on the exact same path.

"She's ... okay. It was hard. It was really hard, Mom," I tiptoed toward a real conversation. I was desperate to connect with her, about literally everything. But she steamrolled me before we could even break the surface.

"Oh, I'll bet! Well, I'm glad you went. It's important to be a good friend!"

And I wonder where I get my avoidance from.

"I'm sure it's nice to be back in your own bed!"

... or your own floor, depending.

"How are things going there?"

"Pretty good," I said, still on the floor and eye-to-eye with the doormat.

"OH! What about that pilot? Any news on that?"

My mom's acute attachment to my success had the severe side effect of crushing my soul. It was unearthly how innocently she could make me feel terrible. I didn't have the energy to disappoint her right then, so I lied a little. "Yeah, that ... I don't know if I'm going to do that."

"OH! What about your friend Julie who's on that hospital show? Why don't you give her a call and see about getting on there! We love that program. You'd be terrific on that!" This is why, historically, I tended to do crossword puzzles or rearrange my closets while I was on the telephone with my mother. I found it easier to disassociate.

"It doesn't really work like that, Mom."

"Well it can't hurt to ask! You never know. They'd be lucky to have you. A mother knows!"

I wanted to scream into the receiver, "STOP IT! Just stop it! Everything is a mess! Ruth? She's a mess! Her father is dead, and Dad will be soon too, and I don't know how long I've been lying on my living room floor!"

But instead I exhaled and said, "Okay, I kind of have to go, Mom."

"All right, honey. I'd pass you to Dad for a quick hello, but ... well, he's resting. The chemo really makes him *sick*." Was this an opening? Did she want to get real now? I was so spent I just couldn't face anymore of this, and it flushed me with guilt. So I told her I was sorry that I couldn't make it home for Thanksgiving, but I was just really caught up with work. And that felt like only a *little* white lie. I mean I *was* caught up with work. I was trying to get some.

I suddenly imagined Mom, Dad, and Drew sitting around a turkey at the dinner table in a corroded silence and I felt sick. How could I be all the way across the country? I kept thinking if I could just get another great job, everything would get better. That was the role I played, that was my piece of the family puzzle: I worked in a cool and financially rewarding job that at once normalized us and made us special. It was my identity and I felt like it was a sort of unspoken agreement between us all. But if I wasn't working, then who was I? What did I have to offer anyone?

"Of course! We understand!" This made me feel worse. She was nothing if not fiercely supportive, always. How could I abandon her now?

"Mom, I—"

"Oh, I almost forgot! We cremated Tigger! You should see the box they put her in, it's gorgeous. It's really a shame to just bury it. Nothing but the best for that dog! LOVE YOU!" And she hung up.

———

I started to lose time a lot. I can't say what I actually did on any given day because I was in this haze, hovering over a darkness that I couldn't quite see but that I knew I was heading face-first into. It was this impending doom over which I had no influence. I didn't eat much. And I started praying all of the time.

You could say that my faith has always been a work in progress. Growing up Catholic and going to church every Sunday instilled a comfort in the ritual of Mass, of devoting a period of the week to God. But the first year I lived in NYC right out of high school was the last time I had been to a Catholic church regularly. I would go to this tiny chapel on Houston Street at seven-thirty a.m. everyday back then. Just me and the nuns. It made me feel grounded. After that, when I got into real recovery for my anorexia, I started to develop a faith that more resembled a non-denominational power-greater-than-myself kind of entity. Then my faith developed into a more Buddhist sensibility, and then a more Universal spiritual kind of energy.

Well, when all of this was going down, I reached out to all of my pilots. Pulled out all of the stops. I was on my knees asking God, Buddha, the Universe, and the fairies in my walls to give me some guidance. I started practicing yoga. I cried through entire classes; I'd be in down dog and I'd have to sit up to stop the snot running out of my nose from choking me. I quit smoking again. And an interesting thing started to happen: I found myself behaving oddly calm in the outside world. I walked around feeling an open-heartedness, a profound sense of compassion for and curiosity about everyone. If you saw me on the street you might have thought I had a freakin' halo. I began to glimpse the massive limitations within life and felt a sympathy and benevolence for humanity. That tenderness was juxtaposed with an instinctive feeling that I was teetering on the edge of a massive cliff.

I think the irony of descending into depression and grief is that it can seem parallel to falling in love: you lose your bearings, you lose weight, you see the world as this miraculous place. But unlike falling in love, you are not heading to expansion and abundance; you are making an undeniable downward spiral, and that floating feeling is just the suspension before the plummet. The calm before the storm.

chapter
FIVE

It had been four months since my dad's diagnosis and although I couldn't bring myself to go back home for another visit, I was finding the distance excruciating and disorienting. I was holding on to the fantastical idea that Dad was going to get better and that everything would go back to the way it was. My magical thinking was elaborate and I was manic. Inconsistent.

I had never really considered myself a reckless person. I mean, sure, I had hitchhiked in foreign countries and been known to speed up when a traffic light turned yellow, and I once took ecstasy that we bought from a woman on a boat from Formentera to Ibiza. (Okay that was pretty stupid, but my Spanish friends felt totally safe about it, so I blame them.) But basically I had always had a pretty solid moral barometer with a clear internal line I did not cross. But fear and grief can make you do some crazy things.

So while I had my halo, I was also bouncing around like a loose cannon. Vacillating between this idyllic sacredness and a dog in heat. I cried often but also danced like there was some ritualistic fire in my belly. I had an affair with a woman. I painted for hours at a time, often through the night, and I am *not* a very good painter. I started an elaborate photo series with my photographer friend Niles. We shot all over LA: on the rooftop at LAX with gigantic angel wings and a suitcase, screaming on my knees in a Catholic church, asleep on the floor of the Beverly Center in my pajamas, lying down in the middle of Sunset Boulevard eating a sandwich and drinking a glass of Chianti, playing volleyball on the beach in Malibu in an evening gown. In my mind, I had orchestrated one of the greatest artistic installations of the century—I'm talking Christo-level stuff here—believing my art would reveal the deepest and most profound answers to life, culminating in a fantastic exhibit that would Change The (especially My) World Forever.

But all it culminated in was me having sex with my photographer friend in a tree in a public park and narrowly escaping winding up in the tabloids. "*Clueless* Girl Goes Wild!" I was just so desperate to move something or someone, to make something happen, to not feel what I was feeling. I was running and running and every time I stopped, I got so sad I almost threw up.

In the middle of this mayhem, I had my first audition in months. And either I just got lucky or this inner glow of insanity was having a positive effect, because I booked the job. It was for a couple of episodes of the drama *Judging Amy*, and my gratitude was indescribable. I rationalized that Dad would be really happy to know I was working and therefore forgive me for not coming back home while he was dying. Like if I worked, somehow it might miraculously take away his cancer. I knew this was irrational and childish, but some part of me clung to that folklore.

My character was "Shelby," a hairdresser and singer who becomes the love interest of one of the main characters. Shelby was in a great place in her life. Shelby was having a blast. Going to set was my secret escape. The cast and crew were my safe haven, my fake family. Complete with its own endearing dysfunctions, but nothing devastating. No one was dying there. Being there gave me a sense of insulation and safety. I felt like this open vessel, a sponge, where every human interaction was so welcome. I soaked up any genuine conversation, regardless of how simple, and it comforted me. Everything felt really deep somehow, really meaningful. Even though all of those people had been complete strangers a week prior. That surrogate TV family felt more familiar than my own.

Every television and film set becomes like a family, and I suddenly wondered about how gladly I had always jumped into those Hollywood tribes as temporary substitutes for the intimacy I lacked within my own. *There's that pesky transference again.* I had chosen a career that required me to manufacture feelings and relationships with people all day long. Yet there was safety in their impermanence, their transience. There was always an end to a TV show or a movie. One day, we all moved on. Always.

So it was the Wednesday before Christmas and my call time was five a.m. I came out of hair and makeup and went back to my trailer to a missed call on my cell from my brother. Drew rarely called me. And exactly never at five o'clock in the morning, so I was instantly sick to my stomach. Dad was dead. I stood frozen in the harsh halogen light of my trailer, amidst all of its mirrors, in my wardrobe with all my makeup on and my hair done, way out in Chatsworth somewhere, and I thought, I can't check that message. I can't listen to that. I'm about to shoot! Any minute they're going to knock on my door and call me to set, and l have to sing country rock songs in a club in front of tons of people. There will be one hundred extras dancing and a smoke machine. And it's the first shot of what will be a very long day. How can I do that if I hear that message? I can't call now...

I stood there immobilized for a solid five minutes. There was a dull ringing in my ears. I was struck by my absurd reflection: frozen, mouth agape, cell phone in my hand, with fake eyelashes on and a sparkly shirt and tight jeans. And suddenly I saw the facade of it all. Then I looked myself square in the eye and had a very simple, lucid, unambiguous realization: this is life. I would not be removing the makeup and wardrobe of my life at the end of this day. My job did not exist in a vacuum. How could I do my job as an actress if I wasn't even in my own life? Not only "What does this scene matter if my dad is dead!" but what does it mean if I can't pick up the phone and listen to this message, no matter what it says? If I could not answer the call of my life, who was I kidding?

So I sat down in a catatonic panic, my heart beating out of my chest, and steadily dialed my voicemail. I heard my brother's voice. "Hey, Wheez. So, just calling to... I miss you. I'm really glad you're coming home. Dad is... the same. Mom is also still nuts, in case you're wondering. Anyway, everybody's glad you're coming home. Love you."

I fell to my knees.

I tried to breathe. I dialed Drew. He picked up.

"Are you out of your mind calling me at five o'clock in the morning while Dad has cancer? Are you trying to give me a coronary!" There was silence on the line for a moment, and I was about to yell at him again, but then I started crying and I couldn't catch my breath. Then the next thing I knew I was rolling over in my sassy pants and sparkles, laughing uncontrollably. Then Drew burst out laughing, too.

"I'm sorry!" he said, "No, really—I'm *sorry!*"

"Please, don't ever do that again!" I sputtered. Then, "God, these pants are so *tight*!" I loosened the zipper as I tried to scoot myself up into a chair. The whole thing was madcap and it was nonsensical that we were laughing like that, but I guess we both needed it because neither of us could stop.

An A.D. knocked on my door, letting me know they were ready for me in five.

"I'm hanging up on you now," I said.

"Love you," he said. We hung up.

I stared up at the ceiling and thought about the distance that fear creates. The tiny fibers it weaves into an invisible wall between our hearts and the rest of the world. Between us and other people, between us and our desires, our dreams. I thought about how many things I had been afraid of in my life, how many other "messages" I had avoided listening to because I didn't want to hear what they might say. I thought about how sad it would be if I continued to be afraid so much of the time that I never really let people into my heart and let them stay. If I never saw that this kind of fear was actually keeping me from having the very full kind of life that I longed for.

I worked for the next seventeen hours, and even though that smoke machine nearly choked me, I was present for every second of it.

That Sunday as I was leaving for the airport, my mom called to tell me that Dad passed out walking to the kitchen and was back in the hospital for what turned out to be internal bleeding. This was not good. I turned back to look inside my apartment just as the door was closing. *The next time I see this place, I will be fatherless.*

Niles the photographer pulled up outside and opened the trunk for my suitcase. The urge to drive away from my feelings was fierce, but we didn't make any pit stops to climb trees. It was clear there would be no more diversions for me, and I sank into the front seat imagining the car driving directly into the mouth of a giant beast.

My mom and Drew picked me up at the airport in Raleigh-Durham. Drew left the radio off as he drove. Save for Barbra Streisand's unorthodox rendition of "Jingle Bells," he couldn't stand Christmas songs, and the Southern airwaves were inundated with them. Particularly those with baby Jesus in the lyrics. The vibe in the car was suffocating: Drew was resentful and numb, and my mom was tired and unsettlingly quiet for the first time I could remember. I was scared and filled with guilt at having been so far away. It had been almost three months since my visit. *How could I have stayed away this long? What is wrong with me?*

"You know we'll have to get home to feed the dogs later," my mom mumbled in an airy voice I'd never heard before.

Drew shot her a look.

"Well, we will..." she trailed off and stared out the window. Drew rolled his eyes.

"Look, Wheez, Dad looks really bad, okay? Like, *really bad*."

————————

The hospital was a behemoth bordering a golf course in Pinehurst. In what felt like an ironically cruel city zoning flaw, there was a workout gym that shared the same parking garage. As we got out of the car I was nearly railroaded by a fit and sweaty young guy with a towel around his neck and a gym bag, yammering on his cell phone.

Cardboard Santas attempted to cheer up the melancholia of the cancer ward, but as far as hospitals go it wasn't so bad. The hallways seemed newly painted or maybe someone had just washed the floor. Mom and Drew stopped outside of a room directly across from the nurses' station.

I walked to the threshold and peered inside. There was this tiny, fragile, very old little thing lying flat out in the middle of the bed and I thought they must have brought me to the wrong room. That couldn't be my dad. This person was an old man. *This person will not get better.* I turned to Drew.

"Where's Dad? Is this the right ...?" His silent expression answered my question.

I stood in the doorway, stunned. The room smelled medicinal, like cotton swabs and death. The blinds were drawn on the window and there was a bluish light flickering somewhere that gave the whole room a sickly and lonely glow. A tube of Chapstick, a water pitcher, and a cup sat on the bedside table. A bent straw stuck out of the top of the cup and it made me think of drinking from a juice box when I was a little girl, sucking on the straw until the sides of the box collapsed to get every last drop. I didn't know what I was supposed to do; I wanted to walk away and go back out to the car. Dad labored to turn his head toward me, his bug eyes straining to see, his breathing audible. And the moment he did see me, his face lit up with this childlike smile. *Ohmygod he's so happy to see me. I can't walk away now. This is my dad.*

I walked over to the bed, leaned down and hugged him, awkwardly tried to hold him. He felt so fragile that I thought I might hurt him. I stayed with my head on his chest, nuzzled in his bony neck, searching for safety. I was waiting for his familiar hug, the squeeze of my shoulder, but then I realized he couldn't move. He didn't even have the strength to lift an arm.

Suddenly we were suspended in time: All of the memories of my life with him, from taking me trick or treating when I was five to sending me roses every Valentine's Day, traveled through my heart. And in that extended moment I just thanked him for my *whole life.* And all at once I thought I understood what it must be like to be a parent; how fierce the drive must be to protect your kids, to want them to be happy and safe. So that when you are lying in a hospital bed and unable to move, you'll know that they're okay. I thought back to all those moments that I had felt my father's judgment and lack of belief in me, like when I wasn't working how he made me feel like a failure—and it occurred to me that maybe I had misinterpreted his feelings. Maybe all that judgment was my own. Maybe he just wanted to know that I would be taken care of when he was no longer there to guarantee that. Then I wondered how I could have let so much go by, why didn't I pay more attention? Why couldn't I have talked to him more, or listened more? Why didn't I ask him why he did the things he did in his life? Why did he get so mad at my mother the way he did? Why didn't he talk about how it felt to lose *his* father when he was only a teenager? Why did he give so much money to the Catholic church? And now that he had turned his back on it, was he worried about where he was going if it wasn't to a Catholic heaven? Why didn't I tell him that now I understood how smart he was, that he was right about business managers and the way I spend money? Why didn't I touch him more? Maybe now I could tell him all the things I never got to say before, all the things I imagined that perfect fathers and daughters said to each other all the time and especially in moments like this.

Then we looked at one another right in the eye, for longer than all of the other times we had ever done so before in our lives put together, and we said—

Nothing.

His lips were so dry, I had never seen anything so cracked and chapped. I took the lip balm from the nightstand and dabbed it onto my fingertip and softly applied it to his lips. I took the hand lotion and gently rubbed it into his hands. I was tender in a way that I didn't know I could be. My mother and brother stood silently in either corner of the room, keeping their distance. *Has no one touched him? Are they afraid?*

My dad looked terrified. I just wanted to put him at ease, to explain to him that this was all just a part of life, and it was okay. I felt if I could comfort him like he had comforted me out on our back porch when I was a little girl while that thunderstorm swirled around us, things would make sense. *I can repay him now, I can be useful.* I took his hand and told him, "You've been a really good dad. We'll be okay. We'll take care of Mom. We'll figure it out."

His whole body tensed, and his bulging eyes darted around the room like there was a madman on fire running wild in front of him. "What? What are you talking about?" he croaked. "I'm not … I'm getting out of here soon. They have to let me out of here so I can go home. I have to hang the Christmas lights and stuff the turkey."

I'm not sure what I was expecting him to say exactly, but it definitely wasn't that.

"Oh, Dad," I started. "Dad, we can do that stuff. Drew and I will do it."

I wish I could articulate the depth and heartbreak of that moment. But I have tried and failed more times than I can count to describe that apex of my fall from innocence. My father's diligent grip on a life that had so unequivocally begun to leave him was a kind of denial that was almost impossible to look in the face.

As if in a dream, I said, "Don't worry about any of that …"

Then I sat there with him, holding his unrecognizably bony hand, wishing that everything going on inside of me could be channeled directly into his soul. Mainlined into his heart.

The ride back to the house was nearly silent. All I said was, "That was awful." I stared out the window at the highway flying by. *This place is foreign to me. North Carolina isn't my home; I didn't grow up here.* I suddenly really wished we were back on Long Island, surrounded by streets and trees and people that I recognized. I just wanted to be home.

———————

When we arrived back at the hospital the next morning, Dad was incoherent and mumbling about being cold and left out in the hallway for hours.

"I was freezing … they didn't give me a blanket or anything … *Jesus* …" he said, still quivering and furious.

Assuming he was delirious, Mom just fluffed his pillow with a giant smile and said, "Oh, look at that delicious breakfast! Is that a hashbrown?" Then she turned to me with a nauseated expression and opened the blinds with a flourish.

I knew his ramblings were probably just the babbling of a sick person, which is typical in cancer patients, but my instincts to believe him took over. And my desire to accomplish something—to actually do something for God's sake!—took over, and I headed out to the nurses' station to ask if my dad had been out of his room at all.

Without looking up at me, the nurse told me Dad had been upstairs for a radiation treatment earlier that morning. When I asked her who had authorized a radiation treatment, she said that obviously my father himself had. This sent me into a rage.

"*What*? He's totally incapable of making that kind of decision! We already agreed that he wouldn't have any more intrusive treatments, that we are—" I felt something harden in my throat and I suddenly couldn't swallow. "—that we are past that point."

The nurse curtly replied that Dad had signed the consent forms himself in front of Dr. Brimley. I felt flames coming up the sides of my neck and into my cheeks and demanded to know just where was Dr. Brimley anyway? The nurse informed me that the doctor should be checking in later in the day.

"I want to talk to her NOW!" I was really revving my engine and pretty sure I was headed for a brick wall, but there was no stopping me.

"Well, she's doing her rounds on the fifth floor."

"WELL, I will just go ahead and find her myself then!" I started for the elevator and this got the nurse's full attention.

"Wait! Miss Donovan, you can't just—" but I was pressing the elevator button, mad as a hatter and that hack of a nurse wasn't going to stop me. "Okay, okay, I'll page her. Please just calm down!"

Here's a little insider tip: telling an irate and emotionally unhinged person to "calm down" is rarely a successful tactic.

For the next hour I succeeded in ticking off most of the hospital administration and a random security guard who I thought was planted specifically to keep an eye on me, but as it turned out was just trying to get to the vending machine I kept standing in front of and banging my fist into.

By one p.m., I had a resident, two nurses, and a social worker lined up in the "Relatives Reception Room." Drew, my mom, and Rita were hiding behind me when Dr. Brimley finally appeared.

Dr. Brimley, who Drew and I affectionately referred to as "Dr. Death," was the head of oncology and would rather have been playing golf than dealing with me. She was a tall woman with a severe chin and a soft, southern lilt, which didn't fool me. When she first diagnosed my father four-and-half months prior and he asked her about his diet, she said simply, "Well Jack, now we just wanna git some weight back on ya. So you eat whatever sounds good to ya, whatever you can keep down. If you like donuts, you go have as many donuts as you can stand."

Clearly a nutritionist before becoming an oncologist, Dr. Death proceeded to tell my father that candy, diet soda, fried foods, and anything processed was absolutely fine to eat. As long as he gained weight, they were on the right track. This, combined with her rigorous and unquestioning fondness for chemo, inspired her alias.

"Well now, your father would like to go home so we are going to start that process for y'all this afternoon and he should be able to go home in the morning," she said, smiling like he had just had his tonsils out or something. Like he *didn't* have a tube coming out of every appendage and orifice, like he *wasn't* on seven hundred different medications that we had no idea how to administer.

I told her that my father believed he was going home to hang freakin' Christmas lights and cook and boss my mother around. I asked her if she had told him that he was actually going home to die.

"Well now, you must be the daughter from Los Angeles," she said turning to me, like I was a fucking toddler. "How was your flight?"

"Have you told him he's going home to *die*? Have you told him that?" I repeated.

"Now, sweetheart, listen, your father is having a hard time accepting the progression of his illness. This isn't uncommon." The combination of pity and irritation in her voice made me want to drop kick her into the vending machine. I plowed on and told her that he had no idea he would be in a hospital bed at home and that we would need help.

"I know this is all very difficult to metabolize," Brimley patronized, with a quick glance to the clock on the wall behind me. Must've been getting close to tee time. "But your father is adamant that he would like to go home."

Come home? How could he just come home in the state he was in? I was almost frothing at the mouth when I suddenly remembered the radiation and I confronted her about it. I told her it was outrageous that she had coerced him into signing something he could most likely barely read in order to fill her quota. She was blown back and insulted at the accusation.

"Well now, just a second," Brimley huffed.

But I wouldn't back down. I pressed her to tell me exactly how much the treatment cost. This question mystified Dr. Death.

"Ballpark! Just take a guess!" I seethed. I was full throttle and it was real ugly. "How much does it cost to fry his insides?"

"Your father has very good insurance and it is covered by—" Brimley countered, nostrils flaring. But I had no time for her excuses, and I cut her off.

"I know that! I want to know how much money this hospital *and you* make for pushing a treatment on a patient who is far beyond the point that it can help him? *How much*?"

An immense pause. Then Brimley regained her stoic stance.

"About five-thousand dollars," she said. And all of the remaining oxygen officially left the room.

"Un-freaking-believable." I stood there almost hyperventilating, my rage hanging in the air like reverb at a Metallica concert. "I hope you get a nice new couch for your office with the five grand!"

I busted out of there and heard Drew mumble, "Wow. She's good."

————————

By four-thirty we had the full rundown on medications, hospice, private nurse care, and bed delivery service. I was aghast at the plethora of pills he was supposed to take, especially because we could get no real explanation of what they were for.

In somewhat of a stupor, I headed to Dad's room to give him the good news: he would be coming home tomorrow, on Christmas Day. I envisioned the comfort and relief I would bring him and thought of how many times he had brought that to me. I thought of the moment years ago when I called him and told him I had just spent the night in the hospital because of my anorexia. I admitted that I had been starving myself for years and was finally truly going into recovery, terrified. He very calmly and steadily said, "I love you. I don't know anything about this thing. Just tell me what you need, how I can help you, and I will. You're going to be okay." And I immediately knew that somehow I would be. As I turned into his room, I wondered if I had ever thanked him for that.

Before I could say anything, he looked up at me with fury in his broken body and sand in his throat and growled, "You left me alone all day. Get out!" His words nearly blew me across the room with their force, like a right hook to my solar plexus. I tried to explain to him that we were just getting everything together for him, to help him at home.

"You and your Hollywood ways, I'm ashamed of you!" he barked. His brittle body was shaking beneath the blankets and his eyes were on fire. "Get out of my sight."

Hollywood ways? What was he talking about? Surely, he saw me. *Dad, it's me! I'm problem solving! Getting it done! Aren't you proud of me?* I felt like I was five years old and just drew him a picture of Bugs Bunny.

"But Dad, you're coming home—"

"This might be how they do things where you live, but I would never do this to you! Never! You left me alone all day!" He was relentless, and it didn't even seem possible that he could have the energy for this rage, but he plowed on. "You didn't even bring me my soup. All I asked for was my soup from home and you couldn't even do that for me. I'm ashamed of you! Get the hell out of here!" *Soup?* His words felt like an electrocution, jolting and sharp. I didn't understand why he was doing this; was this his revenge for my absence? *I'm trying to help you, Daddy!*

My mom must have been standing next to me for at least part of this because she leaned in to me and whispered, "He wanted this vegetable soup. I made it; I just forgot to bring it. I forgot!" She was so disappointed in herself. "Jack, we have the soup! We'll get the soup!"

Then I got mad. Instantaneously furious.

"I'll go get the damn soup!" I bolted past Dr. Death and her team of sidekicks at the nurses' station and out the decorated automatic doors that blasted "Joy to the World" when they opened. I jumped in the car and drove the ten miles home at top speed, fuming, and took the gigantic pot of soup from the refrigerator—*Honestly, Mom, how much soup can a sick man really eat?*—and then jumped back in the car and sped the ten miles back. I ambled as quickly as I could across the parking lot lugging this cumbersome pot that was so heavy and so full, the soup spilled out over the edges through the Saran Wrap that covered it. *This will make him happy; this will prove that I did good!*

I practically sprinted down the hallway and arrived at his room, triumphant. I presented the giant pot like an offering of gold and riches. "Dad, here's the soup. I brought you your soup." I stood there expectantly like a child looking for approval. Without even looking up at me, he said, "I don't want that now. You're too late."

My heart shattered into tiny pieces that scattered all over the floor in front of me. I turned back out into the hallway, still holding the soup. I wept out loud and sat down on a random folding chair leaning against the wall. I imagined that was what such a chair was for: the child of a dying man who just couldn't get it right. I tried to catch my breath through sobs. The nurses looked up at me briefly from their station and exchanged glances.

"He doesn't mean it," one of them said, nonplussed.

I stayed sitting in the folding chair, my arms wasted from the weight of the soup, but I didn't put it down. My fingers gripped the handles of the pot and I didn't let go. I wouldn't let go.

chapter
SIX

Christmas was a blur.

Despite my protestations and theatrics with Dr. Brimley, Dad was sent home the very next day on Christmas morning. Sometime in the early hours I heard the dogs going berserk. I looked out my bedroom window to see an ambulance coming down our long driveway and into the circle in front of the house. I got up and headed outside.

When the medics opened the back double doors, there was my dad: perched upright on a stretcher with a blanket over his legs, fully dressed, with his tweed flat cap and big glasses and a smile on his face the size of China. He looked like a little boy who just got his first bike. The joy on his face as he looked out at the property extending before him, at *his* land, *his* home, with the fresh air in his face, I will never forget it. And I knew the memory of that moment would become a part of every Christmas for the rest of my life without Dad.

It was a full house for Christmas dinner. My aunt Mary Jane and cousin Bridget, several other family friends, and Drew's boyfriend, Beau, were all there. (A quick note on Beau: gorgeous, blonde, cherubic, and twenty years my brother's junior. Beau was the happy-go-luckiest guy you'd ever meet. Thrilled to be away from his bigoted and antigay parents in deep Alabama, he was the kind of guy who brought a sippy cup of Captain and Coke to any occasion.)

Always looking to spend money on frivolous, seasonal crap, Charlotte had purchased new "Twelve Days of Christmas" wine glasses and informed us we would each be responsible for the corresponding verse on our glass when we sang the carol before we ate. Always happy to provide a dramatic flourish, she had given herself the "five golden rings glass," while my father was the "partridge in a pear tree."

Rita flatly stated that she would not be participating in a charade so typical of this family, a family that she still wondered how she wound up in. Beau, on the other hand, was delighted that he'd been given "ten lords a leaping." Mom directed Dad to start, and it was a gravelly beginning. He gave his partridge a humorously macabre sound, like he was gargling a pile of rocks. Then Charlotte conducted Drew to start his turtledoves. After he belted out his verse with fervor, we were back to our partridge, and with a collective bated breath we all waited, praying that Dad would get the words out without keeling over right there at the table.

"…and a partridge…in a…*pear treeee!*" he croaked to wild applause and hoots.

We repeated our cheers each and every time Dad croak-sang his line. When we finally finished the twelfth verse, as though we'd all just run a marathon, we were overcome by hysterics. Even Dad shook his head, laughing at the torture inflicted on us all (but especially on him) by his wife, under the guise of "fun" and the absurdity of the possibility that a Christmas carol could've wound up being the true source of his demise.

————

When I entered the kitchen the next morning it looked like a crime scene. All the burners were going, and ingredients were everywhere. My mom was flustered and manic in an obviously rarely used apron.

"Jesus, Mom, it looks like a bomb went off in here."

"Well your father keeps asking for things, so I just keep trying to make them!" she said, disoriented, like Martha Stewart's deranged cousin that Martha never talks about. She was toiling over something green on one burner, while something that resembled cat food simmered on the other. I opened the refrigerator to find it uncharacteristically stocked with things in aluminum foil and plastic wrap, actual home-cooked food, and it was super weird. I eyed one particularly unusual, round, gelatinous thing on a plate that took up an entire shelf and realized it was a pineapple upside-down cake. I looked at my mom.

"He wanted that last week, so I found an old recipe in *Good Housekeeping*!" she said. I wondered if Dad had become so delusional that he imagined Mom had suddenly learned how to cook. I asked her what else he had requested she make.

"Oh, that Harvey Wallbanger cake, baked chicken breasts, ambrosia fruit salad. And pretty much every day he wants a strawberry milkshake!" she said as she stirred the green goop to reveal something lumpy and brown and unsettling. She continued rattling off all of the things he had asked her to make, and it was pretty ridiculous. I mean, ask Charlotte to make a perfect Manhattan and you're all set. But this is a woman who puts ketchup on noodles and calls it lasagna. And Dad was 100 percent aware of this. She was literally up you-know-what creek without a paddle. This was a learning curve of Everestian proportions. "Then he sits down at the table and says, 'What did you make this for? I don't want that.' And he's really nasty," she said, brushing it off with an expression of insignificance. "I'm telling you, I'd like to choke him sometimes!"

I was honestly shocked that she hadn't by then.

"But, it's okay. I can do it." she said, removing the mysterious brown lump from the pot, which seemed like it might still be frozen. "You know dinner never really mattered to Dad, thank GOD! We had cheese and crackers for our anniversary this year. We had to cancel our reservation at Nina's because he was too sick to go. So I'll make him whatever he wants now."

As if on cue, my father turned the corner and entered the kitchen wrapped in a sheet like a toga-diaper with a deranged scowl on his face. His walk was unsteady, rickety. Mom and I were struck silent. He reached into the refrigerator door I was holding open and extracted a bottle of beer. Then he continued over to the cabinet and took out a crystal wine glass engraved with his initials, a wedding gift. He opened the beer and defiantly poured it into the glass, shooting an accusatory glare at the two of us. Then he turned and wobbled back down the hall to his bedroom, holding the glass of beer in his hand like a scepter.

"He'll never drink that," Mom said. "He just wants us to know he can have it. He's like a child." She paused for a moment and then went on to tell me about the morning of their anniversary that October. She had woken up and Dad wasn't in bed next to her. She looked out the window and saw that the car was gone. An hour passed and she started to get worried, because he had already become very forgetful and should never have been behind the wheel of a car.

"Finally, I see him pulling in the driveway, going about ZERO miles an hour, just like an old person! And he came in with a bouquet of gerbera daisies and roses..." She tapered off, staring out the window at the holly bushes outside, their berries about to fall.

Her face softened and a sorrow came over her. She said Dad had gotten up and driven all the way to the florist because he wanted to surprise her with some flowers. He returned tired and confused but was very serious about surprising her.

"So. Well, he hasn't been all bad," she said, glassy-eyed. "He got me flowers."

Later that afternoon a group of extended family and friends were numbing out on the couch watching football when my dad ambled in almost entirely naked like a stick figure on a mission.

"Who's ahead? What quarter is it?" he wheezed, trying to sound casual, like his bony knees and elbows *weren't* protruding out from the tiny bedsheet he was haphazardly swaddled in.

"Whoa, Dad!" I jumped up and tried to cut him off at the pass. I knew if he was in his right mind, he would never want to be seen like that. He was way too conservative and had way too much pride. But he batted me away with a skeletal arm. As the rest of the group saw him, they were horror-struck and momentarily flustered. Then everyone sort of backed up to give him some room, as though he was going to really spread out and do a dance number or something.

I moved to help him sit down but he swatted me away again and plopped down on the couch, instantly dwarfed by the cushions. It didn't bother him in the least that he was practically naked, and he must've been freezing. Everyone stared at him like a zoo animal, waiting to see what he'd do next.

"Bob Thrasher and I are in this convertible," he said, out of the blue and to no one in particular. "I'm driving. It's a big blue convertible Cadillac. We're driving along and then we start flying." No one knew what on earth he was talking about. To say this was out of character for my father does not even skim the surface of how completely contrary to his DNA this kind of behavior was.

"Oh, uh huh. Okay …?" Beau said supportively.

"Bob Thrasher was his old boss," Rita explained.

"Yeah, like a million years ago," Drew added.

As my dad spoke, he sounded like a mystic telling us a prophetic tale. He stared out into space, smiling, like he was having a vision. "We're driving along … and then we start flying."

"Is this a dream, Dad?" I asked. In a strange way, this was actually the kind of thing I had wished for years that he might do—talk about his dreams, about something other than the very tangible and literal world he inhabited.

"We're flying in the car now. We start going up and up into the clouds. We go up and up." He repeated "up and up" over and over like a mantra, enchanted by his vision. Drew rolled his eyes.

"What happens then?" I tried to get him to say more. I felt like we were close to grasping something very meaningful, that we were on the threshold of connecting.

But all he kept saying was "up and up" and "we're flying in the car." He was totally at ease, as if he was seeing all of us from above and peacefully laughing at our ignorance. *As if he was already dead.*

The idea that Jack Donovan would mention having had a dream at all, let alone one about flying cars with his boss, let alone whilst half naked, was totally off the charts crazy and no one knew what to do. But then it appeared he was done with this portion of the entertainment, and he asked for a drink. Welcoming the escape, everyone else jumped up and headed to the kitchen, leaving the two of us alone on the couch.

I sat there with him and held his hand. This was not easy for me, but I knew I should try. I knew I wanted to be close to him. And I really wanted to know more about his crazy dreams and visions. But he changed topics.

"I like Beau. He's good for your brother," he said with a satisfied and reflective expression on his face. He felt fatherly to me again for a minute, but also like he was confiding in me. *You should remember this. Remember this.* "I'm glad Drew has him," he said. I squeezed his hand.

"You really made an impression on Dr. Brimley yesterday," he said, changing course again. He didn't look at me and was still somewhat staring off into space, but now there was a flicker of amusement and maybe even pride on his face. "She came into my room and said, 'Well your feisty redheaded daughter is here. She's really shaking things up!'"

"I don't think Dr. Brimley is so fond of me, Dad," I said, with a slightly sardonic lilt. "She didn't look too happy that I had so many questions." He still didn't look at me, but I could tell he was getting a kick out of the thought and he was enjoying this as much as I was. For a brief reprieve, we were that father and daughter again: me bedeviling him, him secretly loving it, knowing I was every inch his daughter. We sat like that for a while, just watching all of the activity in the house, and it seemed to calm him. I wanted to extend that moment; I wanted him to keep talking and telling me what he thought, whatever it was he saw. I wanted him to impart his wisdom on me, entrust me with his heart. I wanted to break through this barrier that had been in place between us since forever.

"I'm sorry that I wasn't better at this," I said. He kept gazing out into his abyss and gently patted my hand, nodding. But he didn't say any more.

Beau came in and put a drink down in front of him. "Here you go, Jack."

"Thanks, Beau. Thanks," he said, leaving it untouched on the coffee table. "I'm tired. I'd like to go back to bed."

"Okay, I'll help you, Dad," I said, ushering him up. "You can lean on me." He acquiesced and we wobbled down the hall to his room. From the doorway I could still hear the animated voices from the kitchen—*are they laughing?*—and I felt a bubbling on my insides. That familiar blazing fury that I knew would burst at any moment. I helped my dad into bed, then stormed out of there.

I turned the corner into the kitchen and the words poured out of me in an endless stream of venom. "If any of you want to see him, go in and BE with him! Go back there and sit with him! Don't tell him bullshit lies about playing golf next week and then desert him! Why do you think he came out here half naked and rambling like a crazy person? He hears you all out here and he wants to be a part of things; you're torturing him! You're all making him think he should be well! That he *will* be well! He won't! He'll be dead in a week! Jesus Christ!"

The room was literally vibrating around me; I swear I could feel a breeze from the echo of the air I'd just sucked out of the room. There was a searing silence as everyone just stared at me, the remnants of my blast dangling in the air. Then the last person I would ever have expected to take me on, did.

"Don't you think he can hear *you* right now? Stop yelling! You're not helping!" Rita's head was shaking she was so angry. I had never seen her so forceful and sure of herself. "I do go and sit with him! More than anyone else!"

In a parallel universe I would have applauded Rita. I would've championed her for taking charge. But in that world, I turned on her.

"Don't you start with me!" I blazed. "You just stand around doing absolutely nothing! You're the oldest; take charge of something, would you?"

"Like *you* do? By bossing everybody around like we're idiots? The second you arrive you just take over and bulldoze everyone like you're so smart! Why do we have to listen to you? You're never even here!" That singed me, but I couldn't let it sink in; I wouldn't. So I tossed our entire childhoods and adult lives into the already pungent stew.

"Don't try to make me feel guilty for having a life! You could've done the same thing, but you didn't! That is not my fault!" I knew that was a terrible thing to say to Rita, but sometimes my rage could make me a really shitty person. Rita's expression confirmed my projections.

"You really suck, you know that?" She said, almost swallowing her words, her face crumbling.

"I'm trying to help! Nobody ever deals with anything. Nobody talks about what's really going on in this family! Never!"

"Not everyone lives in your overly dramatic world, Elisa! Wake up!"

"THIS HOUSE IS INSANE!" And like I'd been shot out of a cannon, I busted out the kitchen door and sprinted across the driveway into the horse paddocks, the screen door springing shut far behind me in the distance.

I bolted to the middle of the main paddock, breathing heavily. I opened my mouth to scream, but I was stopped in my tracks by Dibbs, my brother's Hanoverian thoroughbred, standing there still as a statue. Ears pricked and stiff, eyes wide, nostrils flared. That kind of stillness unsettles you with a horse. When an animal that big and muscular, and known for its speed and spirit, stands on high alert like that it is breathtaking. And frightening. Dibbs knew that something was up, and he was on the verge of bolting. He gave an unsettled snort through his nostrils, a sign there was disruption and maybe danger afoot. I locked into his deep, jet-black watery eyes, and I felt my breathing start to normalize. I let my whole body retreat, let my muscles melt into my bones. I slowly walked toward Dibbs and gently put my hand out under his nose. After a moment, he gave a distinctive blow. A big 'ol sigh right into the palm of my hand, signaling he felt at ease again. We were regulating one another. I moved my hand to stroke the side of his face; his coat felt soothing and warm. I slid my hand down his regal neck and gave him a gentle pat. I laid my face against his neck, draping my arm over his back. I looked up at the night sky, black as death, and I whispered, "Thank you for this," to whoever might've been up there listening.

chapter
SEVEN

It was New Year's Day and hospice had warned us that Dad's tumor would most likely burst soon and he would bleed out internally, signifying the end was fast approaching. I thought back to the doctor's initial prediction ("He has a few months, maybe") and I shuddered at the accuracy. It had barely been five months.

Those last ten days at home felt like a never-ending Groundhog Day. Everything just melded together: How long had he not been eating? One day? Four? Did he stop drinking the Ensure too? Didn't we have that episode with the beer glass yesterday? Oh, wait, or was that last week? When did he stop making it to the bathroom? Did he *ever* use the bathroom on his own? I had no real sense of time; it was like we were all sequestered down in a bunker somewhere at the edges of the earth, hunkered down for the tornado that we were already at the heart of.

Sometime in the afternoon Mom went to the grocery store, so she wasn't home when I heard Dad yelling for her. Repeatedly. It sounded almost involuntary, so at first I assumed he was having a nightmare, but then it seemed to be escalating. Rita and I rushed in to find him retching in his bed, vomiting this black blood all over himself and the sheets, like some B horror movie.

"Holy shit." I ran to the side of the bed.

"Ohmygod, ohmygod, Dad!" Rita ran to the opposite side.

I stood there at the side of his bed, trying to ... I don't know what. Catch it, or him, or *just do something to stop it*. It was so black, that blood. Black, black, black and like syrup. His face was contorted, like a twisted Edvard Munch *Scream*. His body was semi-fetal and shriveled.

"Let's turn him on his side—on his side!" I yelled.

"I can't—I'm trying—oh God—" Rita started to crumble.

"It's okay, we can do it. We've got him. On three—" I counted it out and we turned him on his side. His retching subsided, but his breathing was labored and pained. Blood covered the sheets and some of the carpet beneath my feet. I looked up at Rita.

"I think we have to call someone. I think it's time."

———

The hospice nurse arrived later that evening and gathered us in the guest room.

"We're reaching the end of the line here. It won't be long now." She said this matter-of-factly, but it sounded so dramatic to me that I felt like we were in an episode of some hospital drama on TV. *I mean, do people really say this in real life? Is this really happening?*

"He doesn't seem ready to go. Just, like, an hour ago he was fighting me to get out of bed," I countered. And then I thought again. "Or maybe that was yesterday, actually. I'm not sure."

"Well, there won't be any more of that, I can assure you."

"How long will it be?" Drew asked. "I mean, how long will he be like this?"

"It could go on for hours like this, but it usually doesn't. He can't talk anymore, but he can still hear you."

"So what do we do?" Rita asked.

"It would be best to say whatever it is you'd like to say to him now. And if you encourage him to let go, that often helps." She sounded so final, I couldn't quite grasp it.

Mom looked almost transparent, light as a feather, like you could knock her over with a whisper. "Okay," she said, slowly nodding her head. "Okay then."

As soon as hospice left, we went into Dad's room and surrounded his bed in a circle. He lay there at the epicenter of us, his wretched death rattle permeating the walls. Even though he wasn't conscious, he was internally fighting like a champ, I could see it.

My mom spoke first: "We love you, Jack. You can let go now. It's okay."

Then Rita: "You're doing great, Dad."

Then me: "We love you, Dad. Just try to rest."

Then Drew: "You're doing great, Dad. We're here."

I knew this was the last time that we would all be together as a family. It was surreal and sacred, and I tried to imprint the moment in my memory so that one day I would actually be able to feel it.

After a time, Mom went and sat down in the chair at the end of the bed. Drew and Rita went to get some air. I was still bedside staring down at Dad, his mouth agape, breathing with a pained resistance. This was all so surreal, but I felt like I had to say goodbye. In that moment I wasn't sure if it was more for him or for me, but I knew I had to make the conscious and literal decision to truly let go of him. I leaned down and put my mouth to his ear.

"Be free," I whispered. "Just picture bright blue skies, feel the warm breeze. Just float to peace. I love you, Dad. You've been a great father ... Thank you." I stood up and walked out of the bedroom, watching him as I left.

As I opened the front door the cold air walloped me in the face, and I started to run. I ran down to Drew's house and stood in the driveway smack in the middle of all the paddocks, surrounded by the horses lazily grazing under the moonlight. *There is so much space for peace here, even if we can't find it at the moment. Even if we never do.* Even if it was lost forever under that moonlight and that giant sky, and the horrors happening under that roof. *We'll make it, won't we? Won't we?*

"Elisa." Suddenly, Rita appeared behind me out of breath, eyes wide. "He's gone."

chapter

EIGHT

For the last eight years of Jack's life, he and my mom slept in separate beds in separate bedrooms. Mom said this was because his snoring kept her up, and Dad said it was because her reading light kept *him* up. While I can't pretend to understand the intricacies of being married for forty-two years, this always seemed strange to me.

But on the last day of his life, Mom was the one he kept calling for. She was the one he wanted to know was there. He would get panicked and lose his bearings when she wasn't. And at eleven-fifty-five p.m. on New Year's Day 2004, she was the one who watched him take his last breath. And it was not a peaceful breath. It was violent and mangled. He entered the next plane with that tortured defiance on his face, as though he was just about to blurt out one last "I'm not done here, damnit!"

When I walked back into the room, Mom was unmoving in the same chair at the foot of the bed. She was sitting with a glazed and open expression, staring at Dad's lifeless, open-mouthed corpse. It was startling to witness my mom like that. And to be there myself amidst that deafening vacuum that his absence had left in its wake. There is nothing that takes up more space than a body whose breath has just left it.

I sat down next to her and asked if she wanted to go in the living room to wait for hospice to arrive. Without lifting her gaze from my dad, she said simply, "No. I think I would like to stay."

I realized, My God, there is so much about them that I don't know.

Finally, hospice and Archie, the funeral director, arrived to wrap up my dad and take him away. It was odd how I felt this instant closeness to Archie. A person I would know so briefly yet so profoundly as he handled those very intimate affairs in our life as a family. *I am also projecting onto him: Archie, will you be our new patriarch?*

I watched Archie move Dad's stiff and tiny body around. He scrunched up sheets and wrote things down on a pad. And then in the middle of all of this, his cell phone rang. He answered gingerly and I wondered what he was doing answering the phone right then. He hung up and murmured an address to the hospice nurse, and I gravely realized there must be another body for him to pick up. That phone he carried was the Death Phone.

When they were finished, Mom walked Archie to the door like she would have any other guest and proceeded to nervously thank him. And then referring to his phone call, she said, "So you're going to pick up some company for Jack, then?"

"I'm sorry?"

"You're going to pick up somebody else now so Jack won't be alone on the ride?" I was caught between my tears and outright guttural laughter. I mean, literally no one else on the planet would say something like that. And genuinely mean it. Drew rolled his eyes from his perch at the counter.

A generally stoic, and now definitely stunned, Archie paused and managed to say, "Well, um, yes."

And with a gentle hand on her shoulder and an odd grimace, he left.

My mom stood framed in the open doorway of the kitchen watching him go and she looked so small. As the van started to pull away, she raised her arm and waved.

"Okay then … well," she sighed. "Well, I guess that's it." And she watched the van drive away, still waving as the taillights disappeared in the dark.

———

On the morning of Dad's funeral, I was a disaster: emotionally unstable, disheveled, in need of a shower. But I had to get out of the house to the airport to pick up Ruth, who was flying in for the services.

Because of the lack of sleep and the crying, my eyes were extremely dry and irritated. But instead of just wearing my glasses, I was determined to put in my contact lenses. Although this instantly proved problematic, I pressed on: poking and stabbing and eventually jamming the lenses into my eyeballs because it seemed really important to be in control of something that day.

"What are you doing? Hurry up!" Drew barked at me from the driveway.

"Okay, okay, I'll be right there," I yelled, rubbing my eye profusely and stumbling out the front door.

"What the hell are you wearing?" Drew asked, staring at my flannel pajamas with big fluffy clouds and bright purple UGG boots ensemble. "And what's wrong with your eye?"

"I think my contact is stuck."

Unsympathetic to my whining, Drew reminded me that I had to be back before two o'clock so we could hang the photos at the funeral home. "Do *not* make me put those photos up by myself! It's creepy and weird." This was so like Drew to try to pawn off the uncomfortable stuff.

"Toughen up," I told him as Beau and I jumped in the car and drove off.

We were halfway to the airport and I had to stop the car because of the slicing pain in my right eye. I had been scratching and rubbing it so compulsively that the stinging was severe, and the more I cried the more irritated it became, and then I couldn't even *find* the lens in my eye to get it out. So in the parking lot of a Hess station on the side of the highway I finally located the lens, which was in pieces, and removed it from my eye. *Finally! Relief!* But no. That actually increased the pain, and then it was excruciating.

Beau took over the driving while I wailed and cried, holding my hand over my eye and praying for something to stab me in the forehead and put me out of my misery. We arrived at the airport, and I wandered around baggage claim weeping and searching for Ruth, one hand over my eye and the other holding my cell phone trying to call her.

I was in my pajamas, remember. And my hair was so matted I looked like I had a giant Brillo pad on my head. People stared at me like I was lost and a lunatic.

Ruth discovered me walking in circles by the exit door and her expression reinforced to me that I was not fit for public consumption. She ushered me out to the car. Never having met before, Beau and Ruth instantly bonded. They now had my hysterical self in common.

"Everyone is really glad you're here," I heard Beau say to Ruth as we pulled away from the curb. Ruth knew we all functioned better with her as a buffer and she loved my dad. She wouldn't have missed being there for us.

Beau took the first exit on the freeway and miraculously we immediately came to a mini mall with a sign that said Emergency Medical Center.

"Can I get an AMEN!" Beau yelled, careening into the parking lot.

The nurses admitted my blubbering self and laid me down on a table and started flushing out my eye with water and saline. I mean, they were just dumping liquid, accosting me with it. It soaked the front of me and matted down my dirty, misshapen hair, and then I started coughing and choking on top of the weeping. At that point, a small crowd started to gather in the doorway. Then someone entered the room (who I assumed was the doctor but never really said who he was), shut off all the lights, and shined a large black light in my eye. With one quick glance, he told me that I had scratched my cornea.

"And boy does that smart!" he said. Then he went on to say it would be best if I could keep the eye dry, yes *dry,* and that the moisture was irritating it more. So if I could just stop crying, that'd be a big help.

Setting aside my initial question for him which was: If keeping the eye dry is such a priority, why has your staff spent the past ten minutes irrigating it? I instead explained, "Well, I'm trying not to cry, but my dad just died and today is his funeral. So. You know. I don't really know how to do that. And my eye really hurts, and we have a really long drive and we have to get back to hang these pictures I guess at the funeral home? And we don't even really know where we are right now. *GOD* it hurts so much! And I have to take a shower!"

Now the doctor was horrified, like Jeez, who has that kind of luck? But all he managed to eek out was, "Oh. Well, I sure am sorry to hear that."

The crowd in the doorway thickened, and they were all climbing over one another to stare at this spectacle that was me—*Who are all these people? Where did they come from?*—and as the doctor wrapped up my eye with a giant bandage of gauze and tape, he said, "Now there's nothing I can do for the pain, but it should get better in the next couple of days."

In the next couple of *days*?

So there I was: sobbing in my smelly flannel pajamas and dirty matted hair, the right side of my head drenched, nose running, half blind with an enormous bandage like a softball over my eye. That's when the receptionist, who was one of those hovering in the doorway, tentatively walked over to me, and I thought, Oh boy here we go, I'm about to get kicked out of the Emergency Medical Center and transported to the nearest psychiatric facility. But she just stared at me like I was an alien as she opened the *InStyle* magazine she was hiding behind her back and pointed at a photograph.

"Is this you?" she asked. "'Cause when you came in, we saw you and we said that looks a lot like *you*."

I turned my head and with my one good eye looked at the photo. Sure enough, there I was on a much better day, flashing a big smile on a red carpet at some premiere for some movie I couldn't recall.

"Yes, well, yes," I whimpered. "That is me." Then she whipped out a Sharpie and asked me if I could sign the photo.

"Just right there on the side'd be fine," she said.

"Oh, let me just..." and I had to turn my head to the side to *find* the image to sign because, remember, I couldn't *see* out of the one eye. Wiping the snot off of my face, I somehow managed to scratch out my signature with a little heart. Then Ruth rescued me.

"Okay, so I think we're finished here," she said, ushering me out of the examining room and out into the car.

When we finally arrived back at the house, my mom was standing on the front steps waiting for us with a terribly concerned look on her face. As I got out of the car and stumbled toward her she said,"Oh. *OH*... Now, are you going to be able to put on some makeup?"

So at Charlotte's request, I removed the bandage for the funeral and made the attempt to apply eyeliner and mascara to look presentable. I was unsuccessful.

I powered through the service, which was packed with people from all over who loved my father. But I couldn't actually see any of them, and I was trying not to cry because the pain got worse with every tear.

After the funeral, everyone gathered back at the house and we were knee-deep in booze. I was trying to get drunk but couldn't seem to achieve any escape from my misery. Then Doctor Love, our strikingly handsome and notably single horse veterinarian, approached me.

"I'm so sorry about your dad," he said with his smooth and sweet-as-a-mint-julep accent. "I really loved him. You know we all did."

"Yes, thank you," I said, acting like I *wasn't* blinking profusely from the throbbing on my face.

"So your mom told me you had some eye trouble today?" he said diplomatically, like he *didn't* see what had now blossomed into a swollen abscess.

"Yes. I did."

"Well, that just seems unfair. Not the day for that, now is it?" He really had a charm that felt like it could eradicate malaria or something. "You know I just might have something for the pain out in the truck."

"Ohmygod, really? Are you serious? I would do anything."

"Wait right here, I won't be a minute."

Doctor Love made a quick exit and about two minutes and two chardonnays later for me, he returned and pulled me into the bathroom. He shut the door, tipped my head back, inserted one drop into my eye, and I had an instantaneous sensation of *relief*! Immediate freedom from the pain I had been enduring since I began my day, and I looked at him with such fervor and gratitude and idolatry and pleasure that I could see he feared I might just start making out with him.

"Oh my GOD. That is amazing! What *was* that?"

"Numbing drops," he said.

"Why didn't the doctor just give me those at the medical center? That's all I wanted!"

"Well, I'm sure he didn't have any. They're not really for people."

"… not really for *people*? What are they for?"

"Well … horses."

"You just put horse drops in my eye?"

"I've got a sedative as well, but we'd probably have to cut that in half. Or maybe thirds to be safe." Stopping short of letting him shoot me with a tranquilizer dart, I threw my arms around him. And I thanked him for taking away my pain, which was all I'd been wishing for since that whole wretched day had begun.

———

Two days later, my mom and I were standing in the kitchen staring at Dad's ashes in a plastic bag in a box on the counter. We were all ready to go when we realized they don't give you anything to scatter them *with.*

"OH. Well, I never actually thought about that," Mom said with a wince.

"I mean, isn't there some kind of a spoon or a scoop or something that comes with it?" I asked.

Mom shook her head.

So I started rifling through the kitchen drawer. That one that held spatulas, carving knives, broken meat thermometers, and anything and everything else cooking-related that my mother did not know what to do with. I came across two old-fashioned steel ice cream scoops.

"Well?" I said, holding them up to her and shrugging. "I mean, he did always like ice cream."

"He certainly did," Mom agreed.

Rita had gone home to New York to work, so it was just Mom, Drew, and me. Charlotte insisted we bring a camera and all the dogs with us so we could take photos of this momentous occasion and immortalize it. This wasn't a surprise to us. All one had to do was take a look in Mom's freezer stocked full of unidentifiable objects and then look at the kitchen walls covered in framed photographs from virtually every moment each of us had ever experienced, and it was easy to deduce that in our family we inevitably do one of two things: freeze it or frame it. Since freezing Dad was not an option, clearly photographing the event was going to be necessary.

We decided to scatter the ashes from the Judges' Tower at the Carolina Horse Park because Dad was on the board and it was a special place to him. Like his own property, he had put a lot of sweat and time into its construction. It was snowing in buckets when we arrived. We hiked up the snow-covered steps to the top of the tower and took out our ice cream scoops. Mom was decked out with her lipstick on and a cute hat.

"Come on now! Get together!" Mom said, aiming her camera. Drew and I exchanged incredulous glances as we started to toss the ashes out into the snowy wind. Then Charlotte handed the camera to Drew.

"You can't leave me out!" she said, grabbing his ice cream scoop and making a dramatic and graceful toss over the edge.

Click, click. Ashes flew.

I noticed that Drew had some snow on his coat, and when I went to brush it off with my gloves, it turned grey and soaked into the wool. We looked at one another.

"Oh, it's not snow," I said. "It's Dad." We giggled uncomfortably. And then we gave in to the surreal mayhem and soon we were all doubled over laughing. That kind of insanity is 100 percent indicative of us. It's also just the kind of behavior that would have made Dad's blood boil at first until he, too, would be forced to give in to the idiosyncratic charm of this family of his.

Then Mom looked over the railing at the now grey and sooty snow on the ground below. Her face fell as she said how dirty it looked and how that didn't seem very nice. Gone was the congenial smile for the camera; it was replaced by loss and guilt on her face.

"Mom." I put my hand on her shoulder. I told her that the ashes in the snow were actually really beautiful because soon the snow would melt into the soil, feeding it. And then Dad would be a part of the park forever.

"Mmmm," she tilted her head to one side, thinking. But I wasn't sure she believed me.

We stood blanketed in silence and snow for a while. I imagined Dad looking down at us, shaking his head with that irritated expression of "Yup, this is my family." And then that expression dissolved into one of his unique fits of laughter, that at its height had the sound of a high-pitched little kid, tears squeaking out the corners of his eyes.

———————

Scattering the ashes was the last task to complete surrounding Dad's services. It was hard to know when to leave after that; nothing seemed right. My insides screamed that I needed to leave *stat*, that I should have left yesterday. But then an even deeper part of me yearned to stay there forever. Just abandon my current life and let that become my new one: I could move into the guest room off the kitchen and watch my mom fumble around the appliances forever while my brother rode his horses and drowned in Captain and Cokes, hiding from the mountain of resentments he had for Dad, intermingled with his guilt over never remedying those when he had the chance, while we all suffocated in the resounding silence of our avoidance of feelings—

Yeah, okay, no. I've gotta get out of here.

I flew home the next day. I reentered my empty apartment, and what I quickly realized was also my very empty life.

chapter
NINE

In the middle of February, Dad had been gone for five weeks and I wasn't sure I was handling it so well. I did strange things like wander around my apartment for hours at a time, just walking from room to room, trying to find home. I would drive around in my car with no idea of where I was going. And I didn't listen to music. I got really familiar with the white noise of silence. I found myself staring at things for long periods of time. Like at a pencil or a plate. I would stare at the toaster, the windowsill above the kitchen sink, the leg of a chair. I focused in on the fibers of my clothing. I zoned out and left my body when I did this; I went somewhere else, remained motionless at the nucleus of a black hole. And it was almost as if I had gone deaf or I was hearing everything underwater. My inner self was submerged. But it wasn't a peaceful silence, it was a drowning.

One night I agreed to go to dinner with a few friends, and as soon as I sat down I regretted it. They all had a nice buzz and were enjoying one another's company. I sat in the middle of them, but I was removed. I felt tiny and inconsequential. I wanted to shock them to attention, do something to reflect the ugliness I felt inside. But nothing seemed capable of accomplishing such a task, save maybe if I had vomited an internal organ right there in front of them on the linen-clad table.

No one seemed to notice my distance. I wasn't sure if they were avoiding the topic or if it hadn't even occurred to them. They all had both of their parents. Maybe they had no idea what this felt like.

"I really need to say something," I said, lost in the tiny flame of the candle on the table. I felt like The Girl in the Plastic Bubble, stuck inside of it, trying to puncture my way out. My tone must have struck a chord because suddenly everything stopped and the three of them looked at me. "I'm not okay. I think I needed to say that. I am *not okay.*"

My statement suspended us in the terribly uncomfortable density I had created, and for the first time I saw real confusion on their faces. Helplessness. I knew they loved me, that they wanted to help me, but they simply did not know what to say. And then I recognized myself in them: When Ruth first told me her dad had been diagnosed with cancer, I felt so impotent. We had known each other nearly all of our lives and yet I hadn't a clue what to say to her. It wasn't until my own father was diagnosed that I had any inkling of what she was going through. I saw the same expressions on my friends' faces then and I realized we all need instructions. We need a handbook. Not on how to care for the dying, but on how to care for the living who are dealing with the dying. *God, if I could only name what it is that would help me right now.*

"I'm sorry, guys," I said, trying to get it together before I had a high-level meltdown. I wanted to tell them everything, every awful merciless moment we went through with my dad, but it was too much. *I am too much.* I felt the tears welling and the heat rising. Everything surrounding me started to collide into what felt like a cacophonous assault. "I have to go. I'm just going to go."

I pushed my chair back from the table and stood up. I shoved my arm through the sleeve of my coat, but it was twisted inside out and the strap of my purse got caught in the coat and then I was practically knocking things off of the table flailing around, trying to outrun the impending downpour of tears.

"Wait, wait, Elisa—" They were all trying to stop me. "Just sit down a minute—"

"No, please. Thank you, really," I said. "I just need to go home."

"Let me walk you out at least," M. J. said, grabbing my arm. They all stood and hugged me, and I thought I might burst.

We exited the restaurant into the damp Venice air. Two drunk college girls stumbled by us singing Beyoncé's "Crazy in Love," tripping over their own feet. M. J. held my hand and rubbed my back while we waited for the valet to get my car. The tears were really flowing then, and I had to wipe the snot from my nose on my sleeve. *I just want to get in my car and drive someplace safe, someplace far away from this feeling.*

Suddenly a middle-aged woman appeared in front of us, tentative but smiling. Although she was a little blurry (after the Scratched Cornea Debacle I had stopped wearing my contact lenses), she seemed giddy and warm. I couldn't imagine that she was coming over to us, but she did.

"Excuse me," she squeaked, all nerves and flutters and holding up a camera. "Would you mind? I just loved you in *A Night at the Roxbury!* My friends back home are going to die when I tell them I met you!"

I think it's worth noting that this kind of thing seems to happen to me primarily when I am at my worst.

Even though this woman was super sweet, it was totally insane that she seemed unaware that I was weeping. Like big, fat, ugly tears. *Am I on Punk'd or something? Wasn't that show cancelled?*

"This isn't a good time," M. J. said, stepping in and putting a protective arm around me. I looked at the woman and she was genuinely disappointed and perplexed, seemed like a pretty *ideal* time to her. Although I normally always said yes to a request like that, in that moment I worried it might be the thing that finally just broke me.

"I'm sorry," I said, wiping my eyes. "It's not that I wouldn't. I'm just … you really don't want a picture of me like this."

Misconstruing my honesty for vanity, she fawned, "Oh don't be silly, you look beautiful! You're so pretty in person!" She was so energetic and excited, she clearly didn't get that I was upset. While that was alarming in and of itself, did I want to be the one who rained on her Hollywood holiday? Did I want this woman going back to wherever she was from and telling her friends, "I met the redhead from *Clueless* and she was a total bitch! She wouldn't even take a picture with me because she thought she looked bad!" I couldn't believe I was considering it, but I looked at this woman, so happy with her camera raised and I thought, Why don't I just give her what she wants? Give her a nice memory, make her day. Suddenly that didn't seem like such a crazy thing. If I could actually make someone happy for ten minutes, why not just do it?

So I wiped my nose with a snotty sleeve and said, "All right." M. J. was speechless as I motioned for her to take the camera.

"Oh, thank yoouuuuu!" The woman was ecstatic as she sidled up next to me. On impulse, I almost leaned my head on her shoulder for emotional support, as if she was a friend. *I'm obviously losing my mind.* I thought of my mom and her acute need to take photos, like that photo we took outside the airport in North Carolina when Dad was dying, and I realized that in some way I had been groomed to do things like this my whole life. My surrender to the photo had little to do with any professional grace, but everything to do with how I grew up.

"Thank you so much! This is great, just great!" And she shuffled away. I imagined her hanging up our photo, maybe on her refrigerator. The two of us posing in front of a valet stand: her all teeth and bliss, me with glassy eyes and grief all over my face. And I wondered if one day one of her friends would look at the photo and say, "Was she drunk? 'Cause she kinda looks like she's wasted," never knowing the amount of despair captured in that moment. Or how indelibly it would be marked in my memory.

The moment I got home I made a beeline for my bed and lied facedown. The exhaustion I felt was so absolute that I didn't even get undressed. Within minutes, I was asleep on top of the covers with my shoes on.

A cartoon devil incarnate, this guy is. He knows everything about me, everything I do and say. I am a little kid and he's holding me hostage in his all-metal car that feels like a New York City taxicab. He's a cartoon character in a lavender zoot suit with long dark hair and a pointy face. Oh, like a wolf! A big bad wolf. His voice is a vicious hiss as he threatens me: "Don't say anything or you will die. I will kill you. I will kill your friends. I will kill your family." With each wicked word I feel guilt and shame carving itself deeper and deeper into my body. He pulls the car over and Dad gets in beside me. I want to scream and tell Dad he has to get out, this big bad wolf will kill him and there isn't a thing I can do to stop it! But the car peels away so fast Dad slides across the seat and slams right into me. Now we are both being held captive in the back seat, getting tossed around as the car picks up speed. I'm terrified to tell Dad that this fiend has threatened us, so I pretend everything is fine in order to save our lives. Then the wolf devil sends oversized cartoon-like text messages to my phone. At first they appear to be animated and fun and bright, but really they are cruel and threatening: "Tell your father, and I will kill him!" I have to hide how petrified I am. We're heading toward my apartment and the big bad wolf devil starts to unravel, driving erratically at a menacing speed. He is revving up to finally kill us, and I'm panicked, contemplating whispering to Dad what's happening. I need to save us! I rack my brain trying to figure out who I can call for help, but the devil can even read my thoughts: the car accelerates and he texts me "I see who you're thinking about, now I'm going to kill them!" The car swerves violently all over the road. I am nauseous with desperation to save us. But *how*? This has to be a dream, it has to be. You can stop this—

I think it was the terror itself that woke me, because I was slammed conscious as if I'd been thrown out the window of a moving car. My hands were sweaty and gripped tight in fists. I felt seasick, nauseous. *I should have done something. It's my fault. I should have been a better daughter.* I was imprisoned in a twisted fairy tale of my own making. All of the mistakes I had made throttled me with shame and guilt. *I'm so selfish. Everything will perish because of my laziness!* I felt shackled to this dynamic of remorse and fear, like an anchor pulling me further down. Like an old tape worn thin from repeated playing, my guilt slid right into the grooves. *A perfect fit.*

I didn't go back to sleep.

————

Two days later I was on a plane for Long Island to meet Mom at our family financial advisor's office. Right before Dad died, we had a family meeting that was morbid and laborious but culminated in Dad ordering us to "Do whatever Gary tells you to do."

Gary had asked Mom to come up to New York to sign some papers and handle insurance matters. I offered to go with her, because if Charlotte in the kitchen is like an owl at a disco, Charlotte dealing with finances is like a fish riding a bicycle. Dad never let Mom know anything about the finances; he felt it was over her head. With regard to Mom and money, he would always say, "She doesn't know where it comes from, but she sure knows how to spend it."

It had been hailing since we arrived, and just getting to Gary's office was an endurance test I was not prepared for. We crept along on the Long Island Expressway in our rental car, slipping and sliding from lane to lane. When we finally pulled into the nearly full parking lot, the wind was apocalyptic and the hail was coming down in angry sheets. We parked and made a run for the building, our umbrellas useless.

We arrived in Gary's office looking like a pair of wet meerkats. I'm pretty sure my mascara was all over my face and we were literally dripping all over the carpet, but Gary was cool. Gary was a true Long Islander. His presence exuded expertise, but he had that casual Long Island "how ya' doin'" vibe that soothed me. He didn't mince words and his accent always put me at ease.

Mom signed things, I took notes. Gary made calls for Mom on speakerphone so she could learn how to talk to the insurance people and the bank, learn how to ask the right questions. I listened intently, trying to keep a choke hold on this information. I had to retain all of it because I knew Mom would forget. She was trying, but I could see her spacey smile, and I knew she wasn't even listening. All of this was going to turn into Charlotte's Specialty: overstuffed folders with over-punctuated titles written on the outside like "INSURANCE STUFF!!!" These folders would multiply and stack up around the house. And then be ignored. I had to help minimize the number of piles that would inevitably be born of this day.

Some pension policy person asked for the time and date of my dad's death. Mom answered, "January first, just before midnight," and my heart broke for her. Something in the smallness of her voice and hearing her say the words out loud made me so sad. The woman on the other end of the line clicked her keys and typed in the answers, just ticking boxes. My dad had become just another ticked box. I felt a huge knot in my belly start to unfurl, the familiar bubbling up into my chest and the heat flushing my cheeks. I stood up.

"I have to pee," I blurted. I was mortified that I had just used the word *pee* in front of Gary, but it erupted out of me so fast that I couldn't reel it back in. Gary cocked his head a little to the side but didn't miss a beat. Clearly, he was giving me the grief pass on manners.

"Oh sure, it's just outside by the elevator." I bolted out the door and wound around the labyrinth of offices to reception and into the hallway. I leaned against the wall, deep breathing. *I have to keep it together.* Suddenly I had the wholly irrational yet really enthusiastic thought that Gary could come and live with Mom. Maybe Gary could come for the holidays from now on. *Can I call Gary when I need help? I wonder if Gary likes crossword puzzles.*

When I went back into the office, I stared out the window at the ice coating the barren trees. *Pay attention. Be strong for Mom,* I thought. *BE DAD,* I thought.

We got through the rest of the day and Gary said he would stay in touch regularly and to call anytime. *What are your plans for the coming months, Gary? North Carolina is lovely in the spring…*

We stood on the threshold of his office saying goodbye. Gary touched Mom's shoulder and said, "You're very fortunate, Charlotte. Jack really took care of you all. That was always what he wanted, to take care of his family first. He was a great man, and I'll miss him."

And just like that, I understood it. Dad had everything sorted, even when it came to his dying. Our whole lives Dad had been fence building. Just like the split rail paddocks he methodically and precisely built that covered the property in North Carolina. Rail by rail, post by post, while we were all skipping through our lives and no one was looking, Dad was quietly making sure we would always be cared for. No matter what.

———

When I got back to LA, I realized that was the final official business regarding Dad's passing. No more services, no more phone calls to discuss the where and what of things, nothing administrative to take care of. No more distractions from my own feelings. For the next couple of days, I tried to return to my life but I was so lost. Having discovered that I no longer knew how to be around people, I stayed home alone. A lot.

And I developed this odd habit of lying down in the shower. I'm not sure how it started, but I couldn't stop. I would lie there for forty minutes sometimes. I was obsessed with how the water felt pelting the entire front of my body. Depending on where I lay, if I was at just the right angle, sometimes the water almost choked me. I didn't see it as at all unusual or disturbing that I was lying down in the shower and the sensation of nearly choking was somehow enjoyable. More like it was a new discovery and I marveled at why I hadn't thought of it before. I felt comforted by the consistency and the warmth of the water. The droplets coated my face and a body-sized puddle would begin to form around me on the floor of the shower, like a chalk outline at a crime scene. Killing time.

In the parallel universe of my old life, it was pilot season. Pilot season is a hectic and stressful time for actors. We drive all over creation and audition for producers and studios, sometimes several times a day, in the hopes of getting a job that becomes the next Big TV Show. Or at least allows us to pay our rents and mortgages for a while.

While I was taking one of my horizontal showers, a fuzzy memory of a voicemail from my manager crossed my mind. When I was on Long Island angling for Gary to be my new stepdad, Jerry had called about this appointment for a studio test for a sitcom, a chemistry read with the lead actor. *I think that's this week.* Actually, *I think it's TODAY. Oh shit!*

By the time I got myself ready, I was rushing out the door to get there on time. I jumped in my car and headed up Rossmore Avenue. It was a gorgeous, sunny LA day, and traffic flowed easily. Suddenly as I was passing Fountain Avenue, out of nowhere I was sideswiped by images of my father taking his violent, grasping, nearly final breaths. Like an asteroid suddenly decimating me, the images consumed my senses. I blinked and I was back in my car, cruising past the Mobil station and the FedEx. I exhaled and tried to get my bearings. Then I was back dodging meteors. I heard my dad yelling for my mother and then I saw that black blood everywhere, and Dad was retching, his face like *The Scream.*

This is the stuff nobody tells you about. Nobody tells you that, even if you're the baby of the family, you'll have to turn your seventy-pound father onto his side so that he won't choke on his own blood. No one tells you that you'll have to witness your father's rage, be the brunt of it as he curses at you and tells you he's ashamed of you and wants you out of his sight, even as his tiny brittle body can barely breathe. Nobody tells you that you'll want to die yourself, and you'll want to kill someone; that you'll go outside and scream with every inch of you at the North Carolina night sky. And then you'll go back inside and try to help again. Nobody tells you that you'll have to stop your dad from getting up out of the hospital bed that's replaced his California king; that you'll have to hold his arms as he fights you for twenty minutes. Minutes that you watch tick away on the clock behind him. Nobody tells you that you'll have to clean up messes that you didn't know a dad could ever make. That you'll try to help him let go and try to know that he doesn't mean what he says, that he's spitting fire at you because he is afraid and furious and very sick. And you'll want to help your mother and you'll want to stop your father from dying, but you'll want to stop him from living like this. You'll just want it all to be over. You'll want to be dancing in the south of Spain; you'll want to *want* to be anywhere but where you are, but you cannot imagine anything but the four walls of that house.

Nobody tells you that.

I pulled the car over onto the side of Rossmore. I was crying so hard I couldn't see in front of me. I was overwhelmed by all that I'd pushed away, all that I'd rationalized and kept from really touching me. I tried to catch my breath. *Inhale, exhale. Inhale, exhale. I have to get out of this audition. I can't show up like this.*

I grabbed my cell phone and called Jerry, trying to make my voice sound normal. "Hey, is there any way I can reschedule this?"

Jerry's bark was incredulous. "What the fuck, Elisa? No! It's a studio test. They're only seeing a couple of you and it's today only. Like RIGHT NOW only. What's the problem?" He was right. I knew how this worked. I really needed this job. *I can't be screwing this up right now.*

"Okay, okay, it's fine, no problem." My voice cracked. "I'm on my way." I hung up. I wiped my face with a scarf lying on the front seat and checked myself in the mirror. My face was puffy and I had raccoon eyes. I pulled the car away from the curb.

I arrived at the studio and reapplied my makeup in the parking lot. I tried not to think about anything. I tried to just let my mind be empty. I consciously told myself I would deal with it later. I walked up to the building, up the stairs, and strode down the hallway to room H-6. *I can do this in my sleep. I'm strong. I'm funny. This is my job.*

They called my name and I was about to walk into the room when the casting director put her hand on my shoulder and said, "We are so sorry about your dad."

My eyes met hers and my heart sprang into my throat. I was so taken aback by her acknowledgment—*How does she even know?*—by her humanness, that my legs almost buckled beneath me.

"Oh. Oh," I whispered. "Thank you so much."

She opened the door to the room, and I was dizzy. The studio execs all greeted me loudly and warmly; it was a boisterous group. They introduced me to the lead actor, a comedian. He was wearing a baseball cap and some ill-fitting sports jersey.

The comedian and I began our scene together, and I looked at him with pure loathing. *What does this guy know about life? Or death, or anything? What am I doing here?* I was nosediving, the lines of the script seemed shallow and meaningless. *Who is this guy anyway? He's not even an actor. And this baseball cap. I can't even see his eyes—*

"Ummm, Elisa? I think it's your line." The casting director's voice jolted me back to the moment and I discovered everyone was staring at me, waiting. The studio reps looked at me, disappointed and uncomfortable, and I realized I might not be as funny as I used to be.

"Oh. Sorry," I said, shuffling through my pages. The execs shifted in their seats. We began again and I heard the inappropriate sadness and disdain in my voice, but I was powerless to change it. I just kept hearing Dad: "You and your Hollywood ways! I'd never do this to you!"

When I exited the room, I knew two things: I was never going to get that job. And that the worst part of losing my dad hadn't even begun.

See, I had always thought death was this terribly sad, terribly *untouchable* thing. But the truth is, it is *so* touchable and tangible and real. And so *not* funny. And so funny. And so weird and so scary. You are just never the same. The grief had changed the very structure of my face. It was physically altered. I looked for the old shape, for the familiar angles and curves, but I didn't see them. The grief was written all over me. And I needed. *I need so much that I don't know where I could possibly get enough from.* I lied on the floor of my bedroom facedown and begged the carpet for some kind of hope. For some way out of that bottomless pit of darkness that was like trying to push through solid rock.

And I felt guilty about the grief. I couldn't help my father, I couldn't save him! I had no right to feel that lost and depressed. Why couldn't I just get through it? *I'm an adult, I should be fine. My God, help me, please. Dad, help me!* I didn't know how to function. I just needed to sleep. *Please, I need sleep—*

Suddenly I was drawn to my bed. I sat down and I felt a hand on my chest. An actual physical pressure that eased me down to horizontal and told me to *Go to sleep now.*

My eyes closed, and I did.

When my eyes flutter open, I'm floating in a rowboat on a peaceful lake with Dad. The sun sparkles on the water. The light is muted and soft yet bright, shiny. Everything is downy and white. Dad has on one of his velour polo shirts and that, too, is white. Silence. There is no sound here except the delicate lapping of water on the side of the boat. We sit here in this white boat, floating in stillness and bathed in the warmth of the light. There are other people surrounding us on the lake, floating in their own rowboats, silently spending time. No one acknowledges one another, but we are all doing the same thing. All at once I realize:

This is a way station of some kind, visiting hours in the afterlife.

This place is like no other. It isn't in the physical world as I know it, but it is also not a dream exactly. I'm entirely conscious of being in this place. It's like I'm awake. More lucid than I have been in months. I look over at my father sitting calmly next to me, floating with me. It's so quiet I don't know if words can even be heard in this place.

My mouth doesn't move, but I hear my voice say, "Dad, I'm so lost." The vibration of my voice ripples through us both, a pure tone. Unadulterated, like it's been distilled down and stripped of anything that is not me. "I'm scared I can't do this on my own, that I won't make it. Please help me, Dad." I feel my words soak into the core of both of us.

With a soft intention, Dad lifts his arm slowly and reaches out to me. But just before he makes physical contact, he stops short. He keeps his hand suspended in the air, hovering in the space between us. I look up at his face and he's overcome with emotion. He begins to shake, his whole body trembles. And he starts to weep. He struggles to speak, but each time he tries, he quakes and cries. Abandoning his attempts, he rests his hands in his lap and bows his head. I'm unclear what's happening now.

Then I hear his voice in an equivalent pure tone like mine, but it's all his. He says, "I don't remember feeling so much like this … when I was alive. I *feel so much now.*"

Like a shimmering and warm revelation, I'm overtaken by this feeling that I'm supposed to help him. I thought I had somehow summoned him here to help me, but I sense now that maybe we summoned each other.

We continue silently floating together like this for a long time, or maybe an instant. There isn't really a sense of time here. Dad can't look directly in my eyes. Each time he tries, he shudders and looks down at his lap. *If I can just reach him, just physically connect…* I reach over to touch his arm and tell him it's okay, that he can tell me all this stuff he feels, what he sees, and where he is. I want him to know that I will help him adjust, help him to cross over in whatever way I can. I reach out to him from the deepest part of my soul, that place that knows We Are All One. My hand is about to grab his when—

Whoosh. I was catapulted awake, sitting straight up back in my bed, staring at the wall. I was sweating and breathing heavily. I yelled out into the empty room, an involuntary guttural cry that bounced off the walls and knocked me back down onto my bed.

I lay still, staring at the ceiling, and then fell into a heavy sleep.

———————

When I woke up late the next morning, I was disoriented like I had jet lag. My body felt massive and weighty, my limbs like lead. I was mentally trying to metabolize what happened, cognitively trying to put the pieces together, but I couldn't. As primed as I thought I was to believe that there is more than just this physical world, as much as I had longed for some sign from my dad, I wasn't sure I was ready for that. It was too much. It was just too, too much. *And it's not remotely enough! Oh, how I want to go back there! I desperately want to be back in that place with him, floating together. We were right there, so close and it just slipped away.*

I didn't know how to go through the rest of the day, or the rest of the week. After that dream, my life in general just seemed … undoable. There was nothing that could possibly rival being on that boat on that glorious lake together. How would I ever make sense of this life now?

chapter
TEN

It was April and I basically hadn't been out of my apartment since the visitation dream in February. I also hadn't remembered a single dream since and there had been a systematic demise of my grip on sanity. I had a kind of joy amnesia, a flatlining of my vitals. The sadness was like a person sitting in my lap. The irony when someone you love is dying is that while it's painful and debilitating when they're in the process, there are so many distractions. There is so much to *do*. The illness itself is a diversion from experiencing the loss. You are not yet lonely. So it isn't until the aftermath, the terribly solitary time when you have to get back to your life, that you realize the plates have shifted and the floor has fallen out beneath you. That is how I spent those months: searching for earth.

Then on one particular Saturday in mid-April, it was that perfect warm that Los Angeles can be on a late afternoon in the spring, lazy air and toasty breeze, and something woke up in me. I suddenly needed to be around people. I wanted to remind myself that they did exist, the living. I wanted proof that people were out all over the city, that the world continued on.

So I called the girls and suggested we head to the beach.

Driving west on the 10 Freeway, I felt that long-absent sensation of peace and a sensuality in my bones that I get from a nice drive and a great song blasting through the speakers. The sun was setting in my eyes, a welcome blindness. It was so bright I had to squint even through my shades. It was delicious and I felt awake for the first time in what felt like forever.

Windows open, warm wind blowing across my face and the Stereophonics crooning "You Gotta Go There to Come Back," a distinct thought formed in my mind and stuck: *I wonder what's going to happen tonight. Why did I pick this place of all places?* I had only been to the Viceroy once before in my life, for some movie premiere after-party. I hadn't even had a very good time.

The three of us got a table outside on the patio. We sat in the more-form-than-function high-backed Mediterranean wicker chairs with pillows in not quite the right places. I don't remember what we talked about, but I know I was happy just to be there with the two of them. I watched strangers cross in and out of my vision as they moved through the bar. I wondered who they were and what they were looking for, hoping for, hiding from. Mostly I just wanted to feel connected. But I also had this odd sensation of anticipation, like I was on the edge of my seat expecting something. After an hour or so though, I started to feel the heaviness seeping back in and I was ready to leave. We got the check.

That was when he strode up to the three of us, cocktail in hand and said, "Well hellooo, ladies. What's happening?" He had a compact, strong presence; an East-Coast-feeling guy in a button-down and nice shoes. But he also had a slight edge, like maybe he had something to hide. Or maybe he was just nervous.

He inserted himself right into the mix. "What are we talking about?"

I thought, *This guy's got some cajones walking right up to us like that.* He was pretty sure of himself, but he had no idea he'd picked the wrong chicks to try to steamroll with barfly predator tactics. We all just stared at him.

"Emotional politics," I said, to really sound like a bore. "Oh, and the state of Iraq." I was confident that would shut him right down. T minus four seconds and this guy would be outta here. Surely he wasn't trolling the bar at the Viceroy on a Saturday night looking to have a cerebral discourse about anything, let alone war and ... feelings.

"And what are your views on that state?" he asked, "I'm headed back to Iraq for a second tour in June."

You have got to be kidding me.

"You're in the military?"

"I'm an executive officer in the Marines," he said.

My dad was a Marine.

Then I asked him if that meant he was a Republican too. The question seemed to entertain him, and with just a hint of a smirk he said that while the two were not mutually inclusive, yes, he was.

And my dad would love this guy.

"We'll try not to hold that against you," I replied.

"I appreciate the good faith."

"Think of it more like our sympathies," I smiled. He smiled back, a cheeky grin that suggested he was probably a good guy. I asked him what he did over there and he gave us his elevator pitch of what an "XO" does, saying it basically amounted to a glorified desk job with a risky commute. I wondered if this was his personal humility or just general protocol. Our family had close

...ends in the special operations forces and I noticed they were usually reluctant to make too big of a deal of anything they did.

We continued our banter and I realized that I was trying to impress this guy with my intelligence. I wanted to prove to him that I wasn't an idiot. *This feels so familiar. Why is this so important to me? Did I come here for a reason? Who is this person?* I was enjoying the repartee. He was clever and clearly I had misjudged him, as much perhaps as he had misjudged us. It was nice to engage, and I was grateful for the laugh. Then I planned to walk away and never see him again.

We got up to leave and the Marine was having none of it.

"Wait—aren't you going to give me your number?" he asked, almost blocking my way but not enough to make it creepy.

"Look. Even though you're perfect for me since you're leaving the country imminently, I don't do that."

"Do what?"

"Give a guy my number in a bar." It's true. I just didn't do that. Aside from my current state of grief and questionable judgment, I was still sure that meeting a guy in a bar was never going to be in the cards for me.

I turned my back on him and followed the girls through the lobby and out into the valet. They both squirmed and giggled, telling me I should've given him my number. That he was cute and smart, so why not?

"First of all, he's like eleven years old," I said. "And second, no way. I am *not* giving some random guy my number."

"He is not eleven!" M. J. insisted. "Why don't you let someone be nice to you right now? It might be the best thing for you." I let myself think of how long it had been since someone really held me, since I had felt taken care of in some way, and I got a lump in my throat.

As I gave the valet my ticket and waited, I thought maybe I *could* let this guy take me out, flatter me, make me feel special. We could have a great dinner and maybe even sleep together…

…or maybe he's an axe murderer who'll cut me up into tiny pieces and stuff me in the trunk of his car. *What the hell am I thinking? I don't even know this guy.*

Yet as they brought my car around, I considered going back in and handing him my number on a cocktail napkin, just to really seal the cliché of it all. Shaking my head at myself, I got in my car and reached for the keys from the valet. Just then the Marine swooped in and took them right out of the valet's hand.

"I've got this," he said to the both of us. I was a little thrown and a little charmed. He leaned into my open window.

"What if I tell you I'm not giving you your keys until you give me your number?" His compact strength was palpable. His face was very close to mine and for the first time I noticed how kind his eyes were. How handsome he was. There was a warmth and a depth in his smile.

"I could just give you a fake number," I said.

"You could. But then you'd never know."

"Never know what? If you're a psychopath?"

"That, yes." The grin again. "Or if we'd have a great time together."

And then, maybe because my dad was a Republican Marine, or maybe because he made me feel safe (like he could literally shoot and kill the dogs of depression in my head with an assault rifle), for some inexplicable reason, against everything I had ever done in the past, I looked at this stranger and said, "Give me your phone."

————

His name was Milo. We went out to dinner the following week and it was weird. Strangely intimate. Our tiny table at Giorgio Baldi was like a portal to another dimension and we were instantly talking about deep stuff. By the salad we had covered my dad's cancer and his dad's debilitating physical disease that had just caused him to unofficially retire from his job in the Bush administration. By dessert, Milo was in the middle of telling me that he, too, had an idiosyncratic sister who operated on her own program with very little concern for the rest of their family.

"I'm pretty sure she gives exactly zero shits what we think," he said.

Just then, the woman at the table next to us leaned over and asked me if I was who she thought I was. That catapulted me out of our peace pod and back into the bustle of the restaurant. I looked at her and hesitated.

"Umm, I don't know. Maybe?" I said. I wasn't being coy, I was being honest. The second you assume that someone recognizes you because you're on TV is the second they realize they know you from the dry cleaners or Whole Foods.

"Elisa Donovan, right?" Okay, so maybe it wasn't from the gym this time. "We really love your work!"

"Thank you so much," I said.

"Are you still acting?"

Ouch. That stung a little. I knew this woman was kind, that this was a curious and genuine question for her. But as it turned out, it was a real question for me too. Was I? Was I still acting? What *was* I doing with my life exactly? I settled on the answer.

"Sometimes."

"Great! Well, we'll let you get back to your dinner. Nice to meet you!" She turned back to her table.

Milo was lost. "Does that happen a lot?"

"At the most inopportune moments. It's kind of uncanny." I suddenly realized Milo had no idea that I was an actress. I let that marinate and it felt refreshing. "Do you want to go for a walk?"

———————

We lied down on the Santa Monica beach and looked up at the stars. I dug my toes into the sand and pushed my feet in up to my ankles.

We were quiet for a while, and then Milo started to tell me about working the night shift in the desert. He described how vast and pitch black the sky was, that it had a stillness you could feel. He always knew it was the end of his shift when he saw a sliver of orange light start to creep over the horizon.

"It looks like the end of the earth," he said.

"Do you ever get scared over there?" I asked, instantly regretting it. But I really did want to know. How could he not?

There was a long pause. I almost let him off the hook but something told me to wait. Maybe he wanted to answer this question, maybe he was glad someone finally asked. So I let the silence extend.

"Yeah. I do," he said finally. "I have a specific fear of getting my legs blown off. The first time an IED went off in front of us that became ingrained." *Oof.* I tried to imagine what that could possibly be like for him, walking around with that kind of fear daily. *That's real fear. That's legitimate fact-based fear.* I sensed how impossibly inconsequential anything I could say in response would be. I let a long beat pass.

"I wish I had something really smart to say right now."

"Don't sweat it. At least you're not telling me what a 'great job' I'm doing over there and thanking me for my service." It hadn't occurred to me that people stationed over there wouldn't want to hear that. But then I realized it was probably about as useful as someone saying "Sorry for your loss" to me.

"Your parents must be proud of you," I offered. *Why does everything I say sound so trite? What's the right thing to say to someone who's been in such extraordinary circumstances?*

"Well, they can't turn on the TV and see my face staring back at them. No one is asking *me* for my autograph," he said, turning to me with that warm smile. "There's nobility in all things, you know."

I looked away, embarrassed. I knew he meant well and I used to actually believe that about my profession. That sometimes it really could be a precious and noble thing we do, communicating the human condition and making people laugh or cry. But when I got honest about it, I hadn't felt that way about the work I'd gotten to do in a long time. I couldn't remember when I last felt like what I did mattered at all.

"I always thought I would have that big moment, you know? The like, Oscar moment or the freaking Nobel Peace Prize or something. To really prove to my father that I was a success." As the words came out, I realized at once how ridiculous they sounded and also how completely accurate they were.

"Whoa. Nothing like setting the bar high."

"I feel so stupid but I just assumed I had all this time," *And then that time expired.* I was starting to cry then and I had known this guy like four hours. And I didn't care.

"Come on, you're being pretty hard on yourself. Of course your dad was proud of you." He sat up and tried to meet my gaze. But I was out in the waves somewhere, soaring in the darkness over the ocean, contemplating where I would plummet.

"Proud that I'm unemployed, unmarried, and unhinged? I'm pretty sure this is not the way he envisioned my life would be at this point." I could feel Milo holding the weight of my words, but he didn't crowd me. He just let the emotion be there between us for a few moments.

"Well, I don't know much, but I've never heard of anyone on their deathbed saying 'My daughter didn't win an Oscar, she's such a disappointment.'"

"This is not the way it was all supposed to go," I said. And then it really hit me. My career, my relationships, my family—all of it. Nothing had turned out the way I wanted it to and there wasn't a thing I could do to change that past. I considered my philosophy that "The Universe has a plan and things always work out as they should," and it suddenly just seemed lazy. Just a convenient way to excuse inaction as Providence, and then one day you woke up and your life was in shambles.

"I've learned not to rely too much on how things are 'supposed to be,'" Milo said.

"Yeah, the Universe always has a better plan, right?" I challenged, looking right at him.

"Fifty-fifty," he said with that smirk again. "Definitely fifty-fifty."

We walked back to our cars and stood there looking at each other awkwardly. The eye contact was intense so we broke it and shifted around, tried to figure out what to do next. It was like there was this invisible force wafting between us, and it was powerful, disorienting. There was a pull between us that wasn't like chemistry exactly, but it was overwhelming and neither of us knew how to handle it.

"Well this was unexpected," Milo said finally.

"Agreed," I said, looking at my feet.

"Is this really intense or am I having a solo episode here?"

"No, it's happening," I said, still avoiding eye contact. "I feel like I've known you for like a hundred years. So *that's* not weird at all."

"Yeah not at all, no," he laughed. I realized this was the first time I'd felt at ease in a long time. The first time I'd had an authentic conversation with another person where I hadn't felt like all this baggage I was carrying around with me would swallow them whole.

"Thank you," I said, afraid of what he might say or not say.

"Is it weird that I really want to hug you right now?" he said. I looked up at him and realized *Oh, that's exactly what I wanted you to say.*

"You want to hug it out, do you?" I asked.

"Yeah. Let's hug it out." He opened his arms and for a moment, I let myself collapse.

———

This is the part where I tell you that I had grown up and learned my lesson: I did not sleep with Milo. We instead cultivated this oddly deep connection we had as friends. He was literally like an angel that came in to mop up the mess of my gaping open heart that had been spilling all over the place. We had long meals in restaurants where we talked for hours, had lengthy email discourse that was deep and funny and raw, and we just enjoyed one another's company without the complication of sex and all of the mucky intermingling of feelings that went with it.

I tell you this, and it's all 100 percent true. Except the part about us not sleeping together.

Please cut me some slack. I was grieving and I'm not perfect and I was trying to figure my shit out, okay? I was also operating under the knowledge that he was leaving for Iraq in six weeks for nearly eight months. That dance we were doing had an immovable expiration date. I believed whatever we were doing would naturally find its end without any complications or hurt feelings.

Except that isn't how it went at all. And instead things got very messy and very complicated. By the time I dropped him off at Camp Pendleton in June there were many tears, but not for reasons one might assume.

I was crying because of all the places in all of Southern California that Milo could've chosen for us to spend his last night stateside in, he chose the Montage at Laguna Beach. *Laguna Beach.* The place I was still fantasizing about being in … with Martin. *Martin's home.*

Remember Martin? I know it's hard to keep track of the many young lads in this story, but let me refresh you that Martin was patient zero in my catastrophic love life. Our breakup kicked off the entire dumpster fire. Right before Dad was diagnosed. Martin was inextricably linked to my grief in ways that I had not even begun to unpack.

That probably explained why Martin had been torpedoing his way into my consciousness for weeks in an otherworldly sort of a way. Infiltrating my dreams. We would go on adventures together nightly. I looked forward to going to sleep because I knew Martin and I would run wild through hotels laughing, we'd drive along the coast with wind in our hair and smiles on our faces, we'd love each other till daybreak. *Yeah, maybe I haven't really worked through that breakup. God, everything is really starting to make sense here.*

So I drove down the 405 to meet Milo for his final night before he was going to fly off to war haunted by the overwhelming sensation that I would run into Martin. There wasn't a question in my mind, I was certain of it. There was so much I wanted to tell him, so much ground I wanted to cover with him. *But not like this! Not now!* I decided I must minimize the possibility of a run-in by sticking close to the hotel. *Jesus, how have I gotten myself into this precarious situation? I thought I was getting it together!*

In the middle of that thought, Milo called me and suggested we have dinner at the hotel. The restaurant was supposed to be great. Perfect! The gods were with me.

Still, when I arrived at the Montage first, I checked in like the Other Woman. The thought of using an alias actually crossed my mind. Even though Martin and I had not spoken in at least eight months, I wore shades and crept around as if he had spies on my tail, waiting to expose me and my whoring ways. *Because surely Martin has been thinking about me, just like I've been thinking about him!* The hotel was sweeping and stunning and demanding to be noticed. Nobody went there to be ignored. *I am screwed.*

By the time Milo arrived, I had taken a shower and some rationality had taken hold. It was pretty absurd for me to assume I was going to run into Martin there. Come on! It wasn't even in downtown Laguna. What locals would ever go there? Lounging on the beach one summer, Martin and I had watched the hotel being built in the distance and took bets on whether or not it would be an eyesore jutting out the side of the cliffs, interrupting the southern view. I had always assumed we would find out together, that we'd go for drinks as soon as it opened and decide for ourselves.

The lobby lounge was an enormous room with a grand piano at one end and a long bar at the other, all with a stunning view of the ocean. When Milo and I walked in, it was vacant. Aside from the bartender and the piano player, we were literally the only people there. A wave of relief came over me as we ordered drinks. We went out to the terrace and I asked Milo how he felt about leaving. I could tell that in some way he had already left. There was a distance between us and a sense of his being on some mission that had nothing to do with me. Put at ease, I relaxed into the view and downed my wine. We headed back inside to go to the restaurant, each of us stopping in the restroom first.

I fixed my lipstick in the mirror and thought it would be a nice last night for Milo. I wanted him to have fun; he had been such a huge source of support for me. I knew I would miss him, but email would be so much better than the pressure of being in person.

I exited the bathroom and turned the corner back into the bar, and there he was. All the way at the other end by the piano— *facing the other way even, with his back to me!*—and I recognized him instantly:

Martin.

I stood there frozen with my mouth wide open, *HOW could this be?* In a split second I was looking for an escape route. I turned to my left and Milo was walking out of the men's room looking right at me. He strode up and took my hand.

"Let's go," he said brightly, like my entire paper town *hadn't* just erupted into flames around me.

My shoes were glued to the floor. I was still frozen, staring at the back of Martin's head as he chatted with some woman sitting across from him. *Who is she?*

"Elisa?" Milo was wondering what was wrong with me.

"Oh. Yes, ummm," I whispered. And then everything turned to slow motion. Because right at that precise moment, for some inexplicable reason that gives me the chills just remembering it, Martin turned all the way around and looked directly at the both of us. I couldn't actually hear what he said because the lounge was a giant gulf between us, but I saw Martin's mouth form the words, "Elisa? Oh my God, Elisa!" Then he stood up and waved. I morphed my dumbstruck expression into a bizarre smile and waved right back, dropping Milo's hand.

"Martin! Wow! Just—wow!" I mouthed, shaking my head and doing a schizo mime impression of a person who is super glad to see another person after a long absence. And the next thing I knew Milo and I were walking over there and saying hello. We made introductions and the multitude of conflicting feelings I was experiencing threatened to spin me right out the window and into a padded cell somewhere.

"What are you doing down *here*?" Martin asked. It was such a legitimate question that I truly wished I had a different answer for.

"Oh, we're just about to have dinner," I said, like we were in my own neighborhood and Milo was a casual old acquaintance. Like I was about to pat him on the back and say, "Right, ol' *buddy*?"

"Do you live down here?" Martin asked Milo. Another legit question. *Shit!*

"Ah, well sort of close I guess," I stammered, cutting Milo off before he could answer. I should've just said we had to go, but I didn't. Because I really wanted Martin to stay with me and have Milo go to dinner with this woman that Martin was on a date with, *A woman he can't possibly really be interested in, could he?* I felt compelled to have a private moment with Martin, like immediately, so I could update him on absolutely everything. Because *that* wouldn't be inappropriate. *You're in my dreams, like every night!*

Then his date asked if we wanted to have a drink with them. And before anyone else could say the right thing, I blurted, "Well, sure!" and sat down, sandwiching myself between them.

What followed was humiliating. I did not get my private moment with Martin and my efforts to rekindle with him were wildly unsuccessful. When it came out that Milo and I were *not* old friends, nor were we on a first date like Martin and Ashley—*"ASHLEY?" Come on! Really?*—but were instead spending Milo's last night together before he went off to war, the window of my resurrection with Martin slammed shut.

This didn't stop me from calling Martin the next morning (yes, after I dropped Milo at the base) and asking him to meet me for coffee. Martin conceded, and the moment I saw him my confessions spilled out of me like a dam release. I rambled off all of my mistakes and missteps and told him how much I missed him, how I wished everything could just go back to the way it was. *I mean, you feel the same, right, Martin?* I was in a fantasy of magical memory, weaving in every loving moment of our relationship while I deftly let all of our challenges and concrete issues disintegrate into the ether of inconsequential woes.

Martin's thoughts on our relationship, however, had not changed. So our coffee talk culminated in me crying inconsolably as he walked me to my car. I got in and drove straight to my shrink's office in Santa Monica, which was by far the smartest decision I had made in the previous twenty-four hours.

In the period that followed, I spent a lot of time trying to sort through an army of feelings and the longing for a past that was out of my reach. In my search for companionship and conversation, I tried to resist the urge to contact Martin again, even though I held tight to the false belief that he was the one thing that would fix me.

Throughout the rest of the summer, I was largely successful in this goal to distance myself. Save that one wildly unfortunate time that I drove the hour and a half down to Laguna to take a random yoga class and casually stop in to see Martin's mom because, you know, I was "just in the neighborhood." His mom had always liked me, so I secretly hoped she would read the tea leaves and make sure that he was home when I came over. She did not, and he was not, and I left feeling worse than when I arrived.

I was left with nothing but the grief again, and I realized that no matter how fast and how far I tried to run from it, it came right back to me like a boomerang.

ELEVEN

A castmate from *90210* and I are together and appar-ently we are deeply in love. My actual boyfriend, whose face I can't see, comes home and goes to his room to steam clean some of my clothes. He wants to keep them "as remembrances" he says while *90210* and I roll around together, kissing in a bed of ivy that covers the floor. Then my grandmother is there. I am hugging her and suddenly I become very sad. Mom and the whole family are there and I say gravely, "We are all going to get old someday, aren't we?" Now I'm moving through a forest with no shoes on. I come to a large pile, a hill of sticks and grass. I climb the pile and I find a gardener with a shovel. The gardener says I should be careful with no shoes, it is dangerous. I look down and there's an enormous boa constrictor at my feet, maybe an entire foot in diameter and at least fifty feet long. He's intertwined among all of the sticks that I'm standing on, almost indiscernible. The gardener says there are boas all throughout the forest and in the river that I'm going to cross. "You must get shoes," he tells me. But I don't. I continue on to the river and swim halfway across. I stop. I turn around and swim back, then climb out onto the rocks—

The phone ringing jolted me out of the dream, but my body still felt like it was climbing on rocks. *Just put the damn shoes on! Cover your feet! Prepare yourself for the terrain.* I groped around looking for the phone. *Wait. Grandma? And that giant snake.* Between the ivy, the serpent, the gardener—jeez, this was getting biblical. *Original sin? But snakes are also about wisdom and prophecy. Healing and transformation of some kind. That sounds more appealing. I'm certainly in need of some of that. I wouldn't mind shedding this old skin. And while I'm at it, maybe I should take a look at being in love with someone from my fake life instead of my actual boyfriend in my real life; who, incidentally, is steam cleaning my clothes as "remembrances"? Jeez, this is also getting Shakespearean.*

I found the phone on the nightstand and checked the message. It was from Jeff, a producer I had worked with years ago but hadn't heard from in ages asking me if I wanted to do a movie for him in Vancouver. He said, and I'm not exaggerating even one iota, "So it's a holiday romantic comedy called *Eve's Christmas.* It's about this successful woman whose life decisions have left her unhappy and alone. But then a magical wish transports her back in time and she gets a second chance to reunite with her fiancé and her family and fix her life. Gimme a call."

… Hello? Is this my transformation calling? Let me just pack my healing bags and get ready to shed a layer.

Obviously, I was in.

I flew to Vancouver. It was September of 2004 and this was my first job since my dad had died. I was a little nervous because I was in every single scene of this thing, but it was surreal because everything that happened to Eve had a direct correlation to something going on in my own life. In the end of that movie, everything works out great for Eve, so I was counting on her good mojo to rub off on me.

A few days in, we shot a scene where Eve was drunk and sad looking through old photographs and videos from her previous life. Joyous images of her with her family, happy videos of her laughing with her fiancé. The scene culminated with Eve looking up at the stars in the sky, crying and praying for help, wishing she could go back in time. This did not require a heck of a lot of acting on my part, if you know what I'm saying.

And that is precisely when things started to get weird.

I was sitting in my chair to prepare for the next shot and my cell rang. I didn't recognize the number but I picked it up anyway.

"Hey, it's me," a male voice said, sounding like we had just spoken an hour ago. Like I should definitely know who this is.

"Uhhhh, sorry, who is this?"

"It's me, Jay!" He said, sounding a little ticked off, like I was playing some kind of game with him. *Jay?* Jay was my boyfriend in high school and my early twenties. We had made a tumultuous go of it, and it took a lot of time for us to finally shake one another. But I guess I had entered a vortex to another dimension, because even though we hadn't spoken in eight years, Jay sounded like he was on his way over to pick me up.

"Jay? Oh my God, hi," I stammered. "How *are* you?"

"Remember that song I recorded with my band, with Jesse? I just found the CD! Can you believe that?" he said, super casually and laughing easily, like this was our inside joke. Like we did this all the time.

"I'm sorry, I don't think I remember that." I was really trying to rack my brain but I had no idea what he was talking about. *And who's Jesse?* "I'm actually in Canada working right now. You know, it's funny but this movie is—"

"Whatever. I just wanted to say hi," Jay said, suddenly angry at me. "I gotta go. Later." He hung up. *Oh, right.* Then I remembered why we'd broken up so many times. Jay was always jealous with a wicked temper and he didn't like me doing anything that didn't involve him. This was not the first time Jay had hung up on me. *Maybe I just got closure that I didn't know I needed? What is going on here?* My cell rang again. *Oh Jay—*

But it wasn't Jay. It was Martin.

I stared at the screen as it flashed MARTIN CALLING, MARTIN CALLING. We hadn't spoken since the Montage Massacre of June, and I got a fluttering, light-headed feeling of hope as I picked up.

This is where I tell you that Martin flew up to Vancouver and we had a beautiful reunion and he took me in his arms and we lived happily ever after. But I'm guessing you know that's not true, so I'll just tell you that we had a warm but halting conversation. I was starving for meaning, desperate to make sense of things, but we were left with dangling metaphors and hollowed-out hearts. We just couldn't bridge the distance, literally or figuratively. I let myself swim in the sound of his voice even though I knew it couldn't keep me afloat.

We hung up and I held the phone to my chest. Gripped it to my heart.

The first A.D. walked up to me and said, "Okay, we're ready for you."

I got up and stepped back into my fake life, with its much happier ending.

———————

When I got back to my hotel that night, I had two new emails. One was my Daily Zen Thought of the Day, which was "This is not a matter of changing anything, but of not grasping anything, and of opening our eyes and our hearts."

Okay, gotcha.

The second was from Milo. In our last phone conversation, Milo told me they had previously been stationed in an abandoned schoolhouse in Al Kharma. When they left, they gave the Iraqis fifty-thousand dollars to fix the building and be open in time for the new school year. Shortly after its construction, the building was blown to bits and the Iraqi police station less than two-hundred meters away had no idea how. Milo spoke about the door being open for a defeatist attitude when those there to protect the people were so helpless.

Elisa,

This thing is going to take some time and success is not assured. I had a discussion with two of our "terps" yesterday on the current state of affairs. One grew up in the north and is a great guy. He's easy to joke with and will likely be a serious asset to the FBI one day. He says we only really heard about the one time in '88 when Saddam used mustard gas on his own people, but there were other incidents. The other terp is from Baghdad and said things are getting better there, which I guess they are. It's two steps forward and another back though. Another interpreter, an old guy who works with the civilian affairs department, was killed on his front lawn in Baghdad while at home on a couple days off. So.

While the picture may sound bleak, it's good to be here and see the "picture" with my own eyes.

I may not be telling you a lot right now, just know I just wrote an email to about fifteen friends and did not feel compelled to tell them any of this. In a sense I have the feeling that people back home should not know the full story over here, it gets in the way of the barbecues and the ball games. So I tell you, just to help you prep for a light warm Christmastime role, or because our phone conversations have been so strong, or maybe because you are a girl who sincerely searches for the cracked and stilted truth and can deal with it while staying positive. Bottom line, I think you give a fuck and know what's up without being told.

—M

He was so right: both of us were barbecue and ball game buzzkills at the moment. But it made me feel infinitely less lonely to know I had a comrade in this expedition, no matter how many oceans away he might have been.

This is not a matter of changing anything, but of not grasping anything, and of opening our eyes and our hearts. Indeed.

When I got back to LA, it was already October and the calendar was like a map of landmines. My parents' anniversary, Dad's birthday, Thanksgiving, Christmas, New Year's: they all lay out ahead of me like the road to perdition. I felt the darkness threatening to seep its way into my bones and I wondered how I would ever get through the upcoming months. Then like a gift from my psyche, I was offered an indie movie that started shooting in NYC a week later. I accepted immediately and prepared to get back on a plane the next morning. I busied myself with laundry, packing, forwarding my mail. I was relieved to have those administrative tasks to accomplish; focusing on them kept the monsters in my mind from eating dynamite.

By the time I finished getting ready it was after midnight and I fell asleep easily.

I'm standing on the tracks of the NYC subway with a bunch of women. They all have accents. Are they Irish? Then a young girl jumps down onto the tracks with us, trapped, she's dodging the police. We hide her, help her trick and elude the cops, all of whom are men. We start to run and the tracks become a dance floor. Now I'm in a big, open Victorian house. Cooper is defending me from someone who has very savagely hurt me. But his defense itself is so violent I can't bear it. My mom is there and she isn't helping; she isn't doing anything! Suddenly I realize I'm surrounded by a chorus of women. Healers, floating like fairies around me. They're supporting me while I watch. I sense that they're *showing* me, like this has been created for me to see. I'm suspended in the air, perched above watching the battle, like a queen in a coliseum at an ancient gladiator fight. I'm moved that Cooper is fighting so fiercely for me, but he's beating this man bloody. He will kill him. I scream, "Stop! Just stop it!" I am begging. He doesn't hear me. The healers see I've gotten what I am supposed to from this spectacle and they step in and end the fight. I'm weeping. One of the women looks clearly at me and says, "It is the initial one," like that is the answer to something very significant. She says, "Adam. It was always Adam." This makes me weep so violently that—

I woke up in a frenzy, my face wet with tears. I punched my mattress and my pillows. *Can't I just get some* peace! The dream was so archaic and so visceral that I felt it deep in my muscles and tissue. The battle of masculine and feminine, the trickery, the violence, this antiquated fighting for one's honor, and the biblical "Adam." It felt ancient, ancestral, like I was being tugged at by a past so much further back than I could ever reach. And it exhausted me to my core. There was something very important going on, but I couldn't grasp it entirely.

Three hours later, I headed to the airport.

_____

My first morning in NYC, my Mom called me at the crack of dawn.

"I'VE STARTED TAKING THIS DREAM CLASS," she gushed, "So I've been *frantic* trying to have a dream!" Only Charlotte. I imagined her throwing herself into bed at night, squeezing her eyes tight and tossing and turning, "COME ON! DREAM! You can do it!"

My mom and I hadn't talked about dreams since my junior high science project "Dreams: What Do They Mean and Can You Influence Them?", an experiment she adeptly bowed out of participating in. I had wanted to tell her about my visitation dream with Dad, but I couldn't figure out how. It still felt so precious to me, so private. *And what if I say it out loud and then it somehow disappears like it never happened?*

"...Hi, Mom."

"You know, I only remember two dreams in my whole life and they were both in black and white and none of the people had faces!" That content alone could occupy several sessions on the shrink couch. But also, she was literally a unicorn to me. Who only remembers two dreams in their entire life? I peeled myself out of bed and looked for the coffeepot in my kitchenette.

"So, anyhoo! I put that holly under my pillow, like your friend told me to do? And I've got my dream catcher hanging in the window! I'm telling you, your father would think I'm nutso! But I think it's working because...I HAD A DREAM!"

"That's great, Mom!"

"We were outside in the rain on a ramp with all sorts of packages—Oh! I think we were in Japan! And your father was taking me shopping and he was enjoying it! Now, you know *that's* a dream! Ha!" She was right. Dad would've rather put toothpicks under his fingernails than go shopping with my mother. "Listen, I'll just keep you another sec—"

Whenever my mother said, "I'll just keep you another sec," I knew that not only would it definitely not take "just another sec," it would also include something heartbreaking or shocking or both.

"Well, you know that today is Dad's birthday." *Oh Jesus,* I had completely forgotten. I landed yesterday afternoon and went straight to wardrobe. I hadn't even unpacked yet. How could I have forgotten that? "Well, I got up early this morning with my coffee and my journal—you know, I'm journaling now in the mornings!"

I definitely did not know that. "Wow, no I—"

"Oh, I just started to cry. I just got so sad thinking about Dad." She took a sharp inhale and I wasn't sure she'd be able to go on. But after a moment, she did. "So I was lying there crying in bed, and then Zulie ran in and jumped up on the bed. She put her paws right on my chest, and she looked right at me, RIGHT IN MY EYES!"

Imagining that dog's giant paws on your chest was an arresting image in and of itself. But also, Zulie never really cared for my mother. She did love my dad, however.

"Wheez, I'm telling you she looked right at me still as a statue, and a tear came out of her eye! And it went right down her face. She was crying! CRYING! I just patted her on the head, and I said, 'I know. I miss him, too.'"

Mom sounded a little wacko, like Dad was somehow *in* the dog. But I don't know, maybe he was. Zulie really did love my dad. She would sit at his feet when he read, put her head in his lap when he watched television. She would ride shotgun in the golf cart with him on trips to the mailbox. When Dad got sick she walked in circles outside his bedroom and whined. After he died, she dug holes in the yard and lied down in them for hours ... digging her own grave. *Animals grieve too.*

"You know your father really left me with a lot and sometimes I feel guilty about that." That jolted me out of thinking about Zulie. Where was this coming from?

"Wait, what?"

"Well, I didn't really do anything for all of this. I don't deserve it. I didn't contribute." She had never said anything like this before. Nor had she ever been so raw and honest, and I was really thrown.

"Mom, you took care of Drew and Rita and me—"

"Well, I just think about how some people don't have anything at all ..." She trailed off. I saw that bud inside of her that was never allowed to bloom. I felt all that she gave up and I didn't know what to say.

"Anyway. I'm telling you, your father was there with us! And Zulie was telling me 'It's okay, I'm with you. We're okay.' Now, I can't tell a lot of people this. But I can tell you, honey. I knew I could tell you."

We had two days off for Thanksgiving, so I flew to North Carolina armed with the awareness that this was the first big holiday without Dad, and it was going to totally suck.

The second I walked in the door Mom grabbed my hand. "You are NOT going to believe this!" and she dragged me down the hall to her bedroom, closing the door behind us. I had dreaded coming into this room at all. *How can she sleep in this room after all that happened here?* But now that I was standing there, I was kind of relieved we were getting it over with.

"You remember how I lost that necklace that Dad gave me? The gold heart with the little ruby in it? When Drew and I were in Florida." I wasn't sure who exactly she was hiding from, but she was whispering conspiratorially like there were spies in the walls or something.

"Yes, you told me about that."

"So you know then that I haven't seen it since! I wore it down there and then it DISAPPEARED. Eight months ago! Remember?" She was really heating up.

"Yes, I remember you were very upset about it."

"Well. Today. Just this morning, here, AT HOME," and she moved toward the closet dramatically, "I opened the closet door to look for a handbag—on the top shelf, right here—and WHOOSH! Right in front of my face, it just flew out of the closet! It literally flew right past my face!"

"… What? What flew past your face?"

"THE NECKLACE! THE HEART NECKLACE!!" This was a lot to metabolize. Even for me.

"What do you mean? It 'flew out of the closet'? From where?"

"I don't know … from SOMEWHERE ELSE," she said suspiciously, like an aged Nancy Drew. "It just flew right out of the closet, leapt right out at me LIKE A BEAR!"

Okay, so this did sound insane. But I also *really* wanted it to be true. I wanted her to have that connection, to know that Dad was spanning across the oceans of space between worlds and reaching her.

"Wow, Mom."

"I'm telling you! It's like your father was sending it back to me. I read about how this happens. Sometimes objects or things will disappear and then reappear in different places than where you left them! There's a name for it, some kind of syndrome or something!" Then I realized that I actually *had* heard of this kind of thing. Because it had happened to me.

Years ago, I had a psychic named Hilary tell me that my high school friend Shawn, who had passed away tragically in a motorcycle accident when we were seventeen, was currently hanging around my house in LA. She told me that Shawn would do mischievous things like run up and down the stairs to make Zulie bark or hide common objects from me.

"Do you ever leave your keys on the counter and then find them in your bedroom, for example?" she asked. And I nearly keeled over because just the day before I had been late for work because I was looking for my keys, which I ultimately found in the pantry with the Corn Flakes. "He's just looking for acknowledgment. He wants you to know that he's there." And then she said something else, which I had forgotten until this moment: "Shawn goes to work with you sometimes. He comes to TV and film sets with you. He wants you to know that had he survived on this plane, he would've left the town you both grew up in too. He would've followed his dreams too. He's proud of you."

I came back to the present and Mom was showing me the heart necklace. It was right there around her neck.

"Maybe Dad *is* trying to talk to you," I said carefully. "Like he wants you to know he's here?"

"That's just what I was thinking! He's trying to tell me something!" I looked at her and thought maybe we are much more alike than I realized. Maybe inside that fluttery package was a heart desperate to be broken open. Maybe she was as thirsty to unlock meaning and as susceptible to spirit as I was.

———

The rest of the weekend went as smoothly as a weekend could when a group of people put all of their effort into trying *not* to think about how crappy it is. Deftly dodging the emotional booby-traps that popped up all over the house, we also all knew that the real feat would be Christmas. Christmas was the albatross.

When I got back to New York I felt like throwing myself in front of a bus. Or running a marathon or taking up a heroin habit. I wanted an injection of life, of ecstatic life, and I didn't know what to do to get it.

But then at five a.m. the next morning when I looked out at the NYC skyline with the George Washington Bridge in the distance, drinking my coffee, about to go for a run along the Hudson then on to do work that I love—I started to feel extraordinarily lucky. The dawn light was magical and I let all that swirled inside me—the anxiety, the grief, the excitement, the hope, the uncertainty—I just let it all be there and exist together. *What if all of this calamity has actually come to enrich my life? What if I've been running in the wrong direction all of this time?* If I could just put one foot in front of the other, one breath at a time, and Be Here Now...

The city was just waking up.

And maybe so was I.

chapter
TWELVE

It was Christmas Eve and I was deeply immersed in my parents' hall closet, bravely extricating—and in most cases disposing of—objects that hadn't been used since 1982. The most disturbing aspect of this was that my parents had moved into that house in North Carolina in 1994. I'll let you do the logistics on that. Our very first answering machine from the early eighties had traveled a great distance from Long Island to sit stuffed in the corner of this closet beside several dusty Princess phones with their cords tightly wound around them and an original Cuisinart still in the unopened packaging. I had never seen so many half-burnt candles, candle holders, votives, wick trimmers, wine glasses, hors d'oeuvres trays, ribbons, wrapping paper, seasonal decor (Halloween doorstopper, anyone?) picture frames, and woven baskets. It was like Mom was stocking up for the Martha Stewart apocalypse. I also found three nonfunctional video cameras and one particularly unsettling Ziploc bag filled with eyeglasses. *Someone, please, explain those eyeglasses to me.*

That closet had been a subversive anxiety inducer for me for years, silently taunting me every time I walked down the hallway. That closet was also a perfect metaphor for my mother's ability to accumulate unnecessary crap and then shut the door on it. For years she had been buying things to fill a hole of boredom or discontent. *Feeling lonely? A couple of new lampshades should help!* Well, on that Christmas Eve I was ripe for a distraction and determined to throw open the door and kick those ghosts to the curb. *I will singlehandedly dismantle this compulsion and heal her wounds!* I thought if I could tackle that closet, confront one source of dread and unease head-on, my sense of accomplishment would be mighty. I dove in determined to rid us all of this cross we had been bearing for years!

But it became clear that the wrath of woe caused by this closet was felt solely by me. And after several hours of Mom leaning over my shoulder reiterating how much she needed those Santa salt and pepper shakers, I started to lose steam. In the end, I reemerged merely having reorganized the chaos, though the process did seem to calm my nerves.

———

The next day, we milled around the kitchen preparing for Christmas dinner. Drew sang along to Etta James belting "Merry Christmas, Baby" while he shot video of the rest of us. I took the turkey out of the oven and as I put it on the counter, a daunting thought crossed my mind.

Who is going to carve the turkey?

That was always Dad's job. A wave of nausea came over me. I looked up into the lens directly at Drew and he put the camera down. He knew exactly what I was thinking. That was one tripwire that couldn't be un-tripped. We all stopped and stared at the bird.

"Oh," Mom said. "What are we going to do?" As far back as I could remember, Dad used this antiquated electric knife that sounded like a chainsaw. It was this mysterious tool that only revealed itself at the holidays. I instinctively started rifling through that infamous drawer of surprises below the stove. *A-ha!* I held up the contraption.

"Drew? Maybe it should be you?"

"Absolutely not. I'm not cutting up that bird. Not my department!"

We all stood there a few moments until Cousin Bridget stepped up and raised her hand.

"I'll give it a whirl." Bridget was barely five-feet tall so we had to get her a stepping stool from the mudroom. Drew tossed her a pair of swim goggles, which for some unknown reason were also in the mudroom, to use for protection and raised his camera to document. Bridget donned the goggles, plugged in the knife, and it burst to life with a roar. It literally sounded like she was about to take down an oak tree when my cell rang. It was Milo. I took it in the living room.

"Merry Christmas, lady," he said. It sounded like he was calling from Fayetteville rather than Fallujah, the connection was so clear. "Greetings from the other side."

"Hey! Merry Christmas! How's it going?"

"For two a.m. in the desert, not too bad. We all did a shot of peppermint schnapps earlier. That about sums up our holiday celebration. How's Mom? How are you holding up?"

I looked over at the screwball scene in the kitchen and I burst into tears.

"We might all starve! I don't think we really know how to take care of ourselves!" I watched Drew in his ripped paper crown shouting along to Ray Charles's "Busted," swinging a martini in one hand and the video camera in the other, and Bridget in her goggles razoring into the breast of that bird while the dogs ate a loaf of spice bread off of the counter plastic wrap and all, and then my tears gave way to laughter. "We are absolutely nuts and there isn't a thing I can do to fix us."

"Sounds just about perfect from here," Milo said. There was some static on the line. I came out of my spiral.

"How are *you* doing? I guess you're on the night watch tonight then?" I asked, walking over to the window and curling up on the couch.

"Yes. Until four-thirty." *Jesus, brutal.* "I've started to enjoy the quiet though. The solitude is nice." I looked out at the paddocks and the giant night sky.

"Tell me what the sky looks like," I said. There was a long pause, then breath.

"Endless." His voice sounded so peaceful, a whisper across an ocean. "The horizon is like, an immeasurable distance away."

"That sounds oddly meditative."

"Yeah, in a way it is. But it's a meditation in between people getting blown up. Quite the dichotomy."

I am such an ass.

"I'm sorry, that was a stupid thing to say—"

"No, it's okay." Static, then silence. Then breath. "You just can't trust anyone. The reality is, it's like the Wild West over here this time."

"You mean there's a noticeable difference from your last tour?"

"Definitely. The last time women and children were grabbing at us, thanking us, hugging us in the streets. Today is not yesterday." *Word.*

"Agreed. Today is definitely not yesterday."

————

When we finally sat down to dinner, Mom tapped a spoon against her Manhattan glass.

"Okay, people! I'd like to make a toast! Can we make a toast, please?" She raised her Manhattan up to the sky and said, "We miss you, Jack. We know you're with us up there." And then she paused and looked down below and added, "Or, you know, *down there*. Wherever you are! We miss you!"

"Hear! Hear! We love you, Dad!" We all raised and lowered our glasses, alternating between heaven and hell, laughing out loud. And I was certain that somewhere, so was Dad.

————

The day before New Year's Eve, Mom drove me to the airport and insisted on parking the car and walking me in. We sat side by side just outside of the security entrance to the gates. Waiting, not talking. Like strangers on a park bench. Neither of us could acknowledge that I was leaving. All I could think of was her driving back home alone to that house without Dad, alone in that remote silence. I reached over and took her hand; the other one laid lonely in her lap. She looked so fragile. I tried to be strong for her, but I really needed her to be my mom right then too, and it was unbearable.

"I guess I'd better go," I said, standing up. She got up and we hugged, an extended and leaden hug. When we separated, both of our eyes were like saucers brimming with tears. "Mom, I'm sorry I'm leaving—"

"No, no, I'll be fine," she said through her tears. "Go on now, or you'll really make me cry! We don't want to MAKE A SCENE!" she said, with a dramatic flair that implied that might be exactly what she'd like to do.

"I love you, Mom."

"I love you, too, honey. Now, go on, would you please?" She shooed me away, and I turned to walk through security. When I got to the other side I looked back to wave, but she was already sitting down on the bench with her back to me. I watched her and wondered how long she would sit there like that. *It could be a very long time,* I thought.

———

"YOU WON'T BELIEVE WHERE I FOUND IT!"

The plane had barely touched down in LA and Mom was calling me in a frenzy.

"Found what, Mom?"

"The sapphire ring!" she said, referring to this pink sapphire ring that was my grandmother's. Mom had lost it somewhere before we all arrived for Christmas. She thought she had dropped it in the car but she never found it. "Well, I was stripping the beds to wash the sheets before we went to see *Big Fish*. Have you seen *Big Fish*? Oh, you've got to see it! IT'S TERRIFIC!"

"No, Mom. I haven't seen *Big Fish*."

"It's a must-see! Anyhoo, I was walking down the hall toward the laundry room, and I'm telling you I must have walked down that hallway at least a dozen times today! Not to mention, how many times did we all walk up and down that hallway last week?"

"I don't know, Mom. A lot."

"EXACTLY. So I was on my way out to the car and then right there, right in the middle of the hallway, plain as day, was the SAPPHIRE RING! Right there, in the middle of the hallway, like someone just dropped it there!"

"Wow Mom, that is incredible!" I was shuffling off the jetway and heading toward the parking garage. "Did you tell Drew?"

"Well, yes, and of course he told me to 'ease up on the Manhattans!' You know he doesn't believe in this sort of stuff." To be fair, Drew actually did believe in that kind of thing. He just also believed Mom was cuckoo and so he had developed a healthy skepticism of pretty much anything she said.

"Oh, don't listen to him," I said.

"How was your flight, honey? You must be exhausted! You'll get a good night's sleep TONIGHT!" she said, like I *wouldn't* be sitting up staring at the walls of my apartment wondering why I left North Carolina. It was only noon. *What am I going to do with myself for the rest of this day?*

"I actually just got to my car, Mom."

"Okay drive safe, hon! Keep me posted if you hear from Dad!"

————

I dropped my suitcase in the middle of my living room and knew immediately that I couldn't possibly stay there for the rest of the day. There was a stillness in my apartment that actually felt alive, if that makes sense, and it scared me a little. The only way I can describe it is like this: I felt like someone was accompanying me, like an invisible copilot. But I was completely alone. I decided to busy myself. I looked up movie times. *Big Fish* was playing at the ArcLight in an hour. Perfect.

I bought my ticket at the counter with a twenty. The cashier gave me my change and I looked down to put it in my wallet.

Sapphire.

In bold black marker, someone had written "Sapphire" on the dollar bill in my hand.

I was almost paralyzed. I looked up at the cashier with an accusatory expression, like somehow he was responsible for this. Like he was going to suddenly tell me that actually *Punk'd* was not cancelled and this was now the reveal of an elaborate scheme that would culminate in my prankster friends—*and dead relatives!*—coming out from behind the counter and laughing at my expense.

"Is there something wrong, miss?"

"Uh, I—I, yes," I mumbled. "I mean, no. No, I guess everything is ..." Realizing I would never be able to explain to this guy what exactly was happening, I just walked away.

I headed into the theater to watch *Big Fish,* which, if you've seen *Big Fish,* I don't need to tell you is exactly what I needed to be seeing right then. The theater was nearly empty and I had a magical experience watching that film. The main character had a complicated and mythic relationship with his father, who was dying of cancer. Everything from the Ensure in a can on the nightstand to the fury versus the tears, the silence against the screaming, the memories that seemed apocryphal and authentic at the same time: I at once empathized and sympathized and processed my own feelings as I watched. That inner knowing, that itching sensation of purpose that initially drew me to acting and writing in the first place, reignited. *Sometimes this business of show really can be divine.*

On my drive home from the movies, I started to think more about what Hilary the psychic had told me so many years ago about my friend Shawn's spirit visiting me in my house in the hills with my dog, Zulie. She said that when a spirit was trying to come through, if you listened closely sometimes you could hear a sort of clicking noise, almost like a faint crack or a snap. She also described the inside of my house to me, which she had never been in and said that Zulie would chase Shawn up and down the stairs right inside the front door. So whenever I came home to find her barking and bolting up and down the stairs, that usually meant it was playtime with Shawn.

As Hilary and I parted ways that evening, she told me that when I got home Shawn was going to do something to say hello, give me a sign of some sort. I remember I immediately felt a surge of terror go through my body. *Like, what sort of sign, exactly?* I thought. She assured me that he just wanted acknowledgement and that it wouldn't be anything to scare me. *Easy for you to say when you'll be safe at home in your own ghost-free living room, Hilary!*

It was odd though, because I had always thought of myself as very open to this otherworldly kind of thing, encouraging of it even. But then when I found myself faced with imminent inter-action with the afterlife I felt more like, Well hey now, let's not be hasty, I really meant that more in the hypothetical sense. So when I left Hilary and went home that night, I made as loud a racket as I could stomping around. Yelling for Zulie, as if making noise was going to scare Shawn off or something. I kept talking to my dog like she was a hard of hearing elderly person, making sure to leave no space for whatever ghostly sound or apparition Shawn's spirit might have up his sleeve.

After about thirty minutes of clomping around the house, I decided to be brave and just talk to Shawn. I let Zulie outside in the backyard and then paced around the den, wringing out my hands before finally blurting, "Shawn? I'm really freaked out, okay? This scares me and I'm just ..." Then I suddenly felt so silly saying I was afraid. Of what, exactly? I took a deep breath. "I'm really happy you're here. I mean I'm flattered, I guess? I'm happy to hear from you. Just please don't scare me, okay?" Silence. I felt my energy settle and then a sense of almost disappointment came over me. Like I had deflated the party balloon. *What a downer!* I let Zulie back in the house and got in my pajamas.

Then I lied in bed reading my lines for work the next day (we were in the middle of an episode of *Clueless* the TV series). Zulie was asleep at my feet and I heard this faint but crisp noise. Like a *click, click* sound. I couldn't tell where it was coming from, it was like it was just in the ether somewhere. Zulie sat up immediately and growled, her ears alert, which thrust my heart right into my throat. She jumped off of the bed and ran to the top of the stairs and started barking. And then she ran back and forth, up and down the stairs, just like Hilary had described.

Just so I'm clear: Yes, of course I went around the house turning on all of the lights, searching every nook and cranny and making sure I didn't have some critter or criminal inhabiting my home. There were no mice. Just Shawn.

With my heart nearly beating out of my chest, I went to the top of the stairs and waved hello out to the air. When I could finally bring myself to speak, I simply said, "Hi, Shawn. I hear you ... and I feel you. I acknowledge you."

You might wonder how I got to sleep that night, but the truth is I slept like a lamb. Honestly, I was so exhausted and so certain at that point that I was being looked after, the safety I felt allowed me to fall asleep pretty much immediately. I do remember that I was in a bit of a haze for the following week or so though. I can't quite explain the sensation I was experiencing. It felt like a heightened yet softer reality. Something like a floating in between worlds, shifting between planes or something. I know that sounds a little esoteric but that's how I felt. And I wanted other people to know what this felt like too. I wanted others to feel this sense of peace, to be reassured by it. But I didn't know how to communicate it to anyone.

As I got home from seeing *Big Fish,* I realized, *That's the same feeling I have right now.* That's why the copilot feeling was so familiar. I had felt it before, all those years ago with Shawn. I tried to let this put me at ease, but this was different. This felt too close. Too soon. *Not Dad.* It couldn't be Dad. *If it's Dad, then that means he really is gone.*

So I tiptoed around my home this time, as if maybe that would avoid waking the dead. I felt heavy and awful and I was afraid I would actually spontaneously combust if I let even a sliver of that emotion out. I snuck into bed and put the pillow over my head, as though that would hide me from whoever might be lurking around me.

I'm in this strange open kitchen that almost looks like a college lecture hall. One of my punk rock friends from high school is there and I tell him to cut it out, so he walks over to a corner by himself and starts to retch quietly. I watch him as his retching escalates and then eventually he vomits up this enormous, like bigger than his mouth and his whole body, frog-monster thing. It is maroon in color and has webbed feet, resembling an enormous brick-red flat frog. I watch this creature slither by me and out into the street. Then it slides down the grate in the pavement into the sewer and I think, *"Oh no! Now everything is poisoned. He has infiltrated our system. He will now color everything, get into our water. He will make us all sick!"* Then I'm standing face to face with another woman, as if in a mirror. I'm saying, "Wait, I have to remember this? I have to remember this. I won't, I don't want to remember this. This is not the dream I want to have!" And I try to convince this other woman, this reflection of me. This is not—

I was jolted awake yelling, "This is not the dream I want!" I looked around my bedroom to get my bearings. I reached for the full glass of water on my nightstand, knocking it over. The water spilled everywhere, soaking my journal and my alarm clock and my slippers on the carpet. *Shiiiiiiiiiiit!*

This is not the dream I want. Ha. What an understatement. Was I that afraid of my feelings? Could I not even look in a mirror without screaming that I didn't want what was looking back at me? Was I telling my creativity and my feelings to "cut it out" because they would poison everything? Even if tomorrow was New Year's Day and I *was* trying to figure out how to transport myself directly to January 2 and bypass it altogether, would a slithery frog monster vomit itself all over the rug if I didn't? *Where are you, Dad? Where did you go?*

Suddenly I thought of Hilary and Shawn again. And then I remembered my friend Matt. Matt and Shawn had been very close friends, much closer than I had ever been to Shawn myself. At one point in our time together, Hilary the psychic asked me if I had any questions for Shawn. I thought of Matt and asked if Shawn had any message for him. She paused for several moments and then said, "Shawn says he visits Matt when he sleeps. They go on long walks together." She went on to tell me that Shawn came to Matt in his dreams and they spent time walking in peaceful, familiar places. Shawn reassured Matt on these walks, helped him with his sadness. Hilary said it might be too much for Matt to talk about, so I should be gentle in broaching the subject with him. In that hazy aftermath of days, I eventually called Matt and left him a voicemail sharing all that Hilary had told me.

Matt called me back later and said he didn't remember any sort of dream with Shawn, but that it made him happy to imagine it. Then, he said that immediately after he listened to my message, the urge to write a song came over him. He was standing in his kitchen with the refrigerator door open when he was compelled to pick up his guitar and start playing. The lyrics and the melody came out of him instantaneously. He went on to play the song for me over the telephone and I started to cry. I wish you could hear Matt's voice and his guitar through this page because they are haunting and beautiful.

Dear Waiting Coincidence

This is a message that's old and out of date
    Well I got your dead letter from the post office
    And I read the words of you, my friend.
    And you look like someone who liked who they are
    But you don't strike me as
    Someone who's made by chance,
    Someone who's made by accident.

Well I heard you've been comin' when I've been sleeping

And she said you talk, you talk to me, you say it's gonna be alright

And Zulie and Lisa hear you laughing and hear you playing

She says she talks, she talks to you, but we're not really sure you're there.

Gone, gone away

But I got your better days, I got your better days.

And you look like someone who likes who they are

But you don't strike me as someone who's made by chance,

Someone who's made by accident.

I'm sorry you died by chance,

You were only living by accident.

Matt said he had never written something like that before and certainly never so fast. He had no idea what was happening and was glad that he recorded it immediately because he didn't know if he would have been able to play it again otherwise. I recounted Hilary saying that if Shawn had survived on this plane, he would have "followed his dreams too," and I wondered if this was somehow his way of finally doing that.

How could I have forgotten about all of this? I thought about my visitation dream with Dad, almost a year ago at that point, and I missed it with a drowning desperation. But I also felt grateful that I had the memory at all, that my consciousness allowed me to be "awake" for it. I was struck by the varying ways we are touched by those we love and who love us, the great distances and dimensions our bonds can cross.

————

Despite my attempts at teleporting to January 2, January 1 arrived on schedule and with an unrivaled lethargy.

Happy 2005.

Happy one year anniversary of Dad's death.

Mom and I spoke briefly that morning. We were all just waiting for the day to be over so we would know that we had survived it. Had it behind us. *Come on. It's just a day. Like any other day.*

Except it wasn't. And it never would be.

And what if that was exactly the point?

Everything *had* changed and things would never be the same. Okay. So.

I thought about an email exchange between Milo and me from a couple of weeks back. Milo shared a story about a young soldier in his battalion who watched one of their superior officers be shot dead in front of him during a surprise attack in the middle of the night. Milo said he usually tried to look at much of what he's going through over there as a "rite of passage" of sorts.

"But it's a rite of passage in which people get blown the fuck up," he said. "I guess if I think about it, my worldviews are getting shaped, at least a baseline to work from. Most people have worldviews and don't have a whole heck of a lot to base them on, so I guess I've got that going for me. Sometimes people like to associate themselves with tragedy, like after the World Trade Center bombings. To get closer to the experience."

I agreed with him. People did often want to associate themselves to tragic events like that; like if they were closely connected it made them feel included and meaningful, or at least justified their need to talk about it. I supposed we are all guilty of doing that to some degree, in some way, at one time or another. Whether it was rubbernecking at a car accident or watching a fight on the playground when you were ten. But I realized then that when you're in direct proximity to it, when you are an integral element of the tragedy, conversely, a large part of you wants to forget you were ever there. I told him I was pretty sure that soldier would gladly give up that experience in exchange for having nothing to say about it. But the reality is, he can't. It happened, and it happened to *him*. And he will never be the same because of it.

While what I had gone through in the previous eighteen months was certainly not comparable to a literal war, those things had unequivocally shaped who I now was. So I was faced with a question: was I going to let those things shape me for the better?

chapter
THIRTEEN

This may not come as a surprise, but Jack Donovan was not a fan of mohawk haircuts. Ditto for black nail polish, chained wallets, combat boots, or concert T-shirts with cartoons of men peeing into toilets (all of which my boyfriends in junior high and high school wore regularly). And although the word *boyfriend* (much like the words *menstruation*, *sex*, and *puberty*) wasn't spoken in our house, I did bring boys over once in a while. Like Nick, for example. Nick was a painter and a skateboarder in the eighth grade with a stiff and impressive twelve-inch mohawk standing atop his head. When Nick came over for dinner, all the conversation Jack could muster was, "So, how do you keep that thing standing, son?" To which Nick responded, with his only words for the evening, "Elmer's Glue."

It's safe to say that Mohawk Nick and Milo would not have been friends in high school. And I needed to admit I'd been fantasizing that when Milo returned we would have a family dinner where Dad was finally able to have a conversation with a boyfriend of mine that he could actually understand. I had imagined Dad being proud of Milo (and of me for bringing him to the table). I had pictured them laughing at the same jokes and the three of us having an animated but friendly discussion about politics into the wee hours.

To use Drew's language, this was the crux of the biscuit. Milo and I definitely had an otherworldly sort of connection, and our letters to one another, both digital and handwritten, had kept me afloat those last eight months. But I also knew that a giant undercurrent of our relationship for me was how much my dad would've loved him. And I knew that I had to start taking a real responsibility for my part in these liaisons.

Milo got home in mid-January and my anticipation was only matched by my dread. Part of me could not wait and imagined us diving into one another's arms and never letting go. Another part of me wanted to run screaming in the opposite direction. And a third magical-thinking part of me wondered why we couldn't just keep writing letters to each other and have long distance phone sessions. Why not?

I will spare you the uncomfortable details, but I told Milo that I didn't think it was going to work between us, and our intricate relationship started to unravel. Even though he kicked and screamed a little, the truth is that he wasn't really ready for the serious kind of relationship that we would certainly have been having if we had stayed together. Milo just wasn't there. He was younger than I was and had his own set of things he needed to go through. But we couldn't quite disentangle ourselves from one another; the tentacles of our connection were sinewy and slippery. It was a messy and lingering end, and it took over a year for us to really separate. We both accepted that this kinship and affinity for one another was complicated and difficult to extricate ourselves from. More than once (maybe several *hundred* times),

I wondered how things might have wound up if we had never crossed the line from friendship into romance, reminding myself that the only reason we needed to disentangle ourselves at all is because we complicated things with the physical. We came to the conclusion that this bond we had was both literal—Milo admitted that my letters got him through the previous year just as much as his helped me—and otherworldly. We had probably known one another in a past life and maybe that's why we didn't want to desert each other in this one. We agreed that most likely we had "been through some gnarly shit together" at some point and felt deeply protective of one another. While this may seem like a clean or lazy (or maybe even *banana-town-crazy*) excuse for the dynamics of our relationship, it was not an explanation that we came to easily or simply. But it did reinforce to me that there are angels among us. And Milo was one of them.

The day that we officially agreed to let one another go, I had an appointment with a psychic named Teresa whom I had never met before. We had barely greeted one another when Teresa launched in, telling me I was in a karmic relationship and there was much struggle around it, but I shouldn't try to force something to make it fit. She told me this man and I were catalysts for one another and that I was learning about powerlessness and Milo was learning his own lessons. She said we were on different pages and that karmic relationships needed to play themselves out or they would keep coming back. I marveled at her accuracy. And I wondered what I would have thought if I had come for the reading a year ago when Milo had just gotten home from Iraq. Would it have changed anything?

Then Teresa asked me if it was okay if she gave me a message from my father.

The first thing she told me was what a big heart my dad had. She said he was showing her that he and I connected very strongly once he wasn't well. And that now in death, he could express his affection and love in a way he couldn't on this plane. She told me this life hadn't been an easy path for him.

"He didn't have a passion for what he did, he wanted the country. He wanted to work the land and be outside." I had never really thought about whether or not Dad was "passionate" about his work. *Did I assume that passion for one's work was a luxury only I was afforded? Did I assume he had no passion at all?* What must it have been like to spend the majority of his life doing something he didn't enjoy just to provide for us? I thought of all of those summers growing up on Long Island. After his hectic work week in the city, Dad would sometimes spend entire weekends planting and tending to his vegetable garden that grew tomatoes and zucchinis the size of watermelons. He would grill steaks and baked clams and corn on the cob. He landscaped our whole backyard himself: Japanese maple trees, rock gardens, marigolds, rose bushes, and vines that crawled up the surrounding fence. I suddenly had a new compassion for him and an even greater gratitude for the sacrifices he must have made for us.

"He's complete on the other side though. He is whole now," Teresa said. Her words were so succinct and she said them with such simplicity, it was jarring. Yet they resonated. *Of course he is. That makes so much sense.*

"He's around you now and feels sorry that he couldn't do that when he was here. He also wants you to make the connection between Milo and himself. How emotionally alike they are." This confused me at first but then it settled in: as much as I couldn't articulate the complexity of my feelings to Milo, Milo also couldn't just dive in and express his to me either.

Then she said that the book I was writing was very important because I could help people by sharing what I went through. I was stunned because, indeed, I had started putting together some of my writing from this time and always wanted to write a book but had no idea what to do with it. My self-doubt always got in the way. *How can I write a book? How will I ever get a book published?*

"You have success and sincerity in your heart, and you must move forward with this." Then she laughed and said that my dad was showing her a single rose and a plaque of some kind, which he would like to be on the cover of the book. "He's very pushy, your father. What a funny man!" I was stopped in my tracks as I recalled a photograph my mom had taken on my last visit to North Carolina. It was a closeup of me *holding a rose in front of a plaque* dedicating a fence at the horse park to my father.

Then Teresa told me that I've been on a learning curve and that a learning curve is not always a straight path. *Well, that's an understatement.* She said, "Harness the abilities that you've forgotten you have. It is time to take an empty-handed leap and trust."

———

I started to see signs from Dad everywhere.

I went into a bookstore to buy Joan Didion's *The Year of Magical Thinking* (the book about mourning the loss of her husband and child) and suddenly Louis Armstrong bellowed through the speakers. I received a piece of fan mail that was a laminated photograph of a butterfly and a flowering tree branch with a note saying, "I read that your late father used to send you roses every year on your birthday. Because we are strangers I can't do that but I hope you like this photograph of a western tiger swallow on a

Jacaranda branch that I took. Happy Birthday!" The handwriting had an odd resemblance to my dad's chicken scratch.

I felt lonely at nighttime and often couldn't sleep. One night, I opened my nightstand and took out a book of *New York Times* crossword puzzles. Doing a crossword always worked my mind in just the right way to distract me from the vicious cycle of my thoughts, while also giving me a sense of accomplishment so I could drift off to sleep. I opened to a random page and there was my dad's undeniable writing. His tiny crooked lettering that looked like the work of a madman or maybe a brain surgeon. I was so arrested by the sight of his distinctive hand that it took my breath away. *I must have taken one of Dad's crossword books and put it in my nightstand at some point, some time… I guess?*

That summer I booked a movie where my character reestablishes her relationship with her estranged father. On my first day, they were doing construction on one of the sets and there was a big piece of lumber strewn across a sawhorse with the words "CAPTAIN JACK" inexplicably stenciled across it in all caps. All the movement around me went into slow motion as I stood there staring at this piece of wood. I was stunned. And then I started to laugh. *I guess Dad would like us to know who exactly is running things here.* I went to hair and makeup to meet Tom Skerritt, the actor who was playing my father. He was the gentlest of souls and he took my hand in his and just held it. He looked in my eyes and with the sweetest of smiles said, "It's nice to meet you, kiddo." *Kiddo. That's what Dad always called me.* I was so overcome by emotion that I couldn't say anything, so I just leaned in and hugged him.

That fall I was driving on the 101 en route to a meeting for a film. I had zero interest in doing the movie, but they were going to pay me well and I needed to work, so I took the meeting. The script was so bad I couldn't even get through the first ten pages. I was judging myself and the state of my life. How was I going to shoot a film that I couldn't even get through the script of? I started to feel heavy, melancholic. The surface of the freeway in front of me disappeared under the hood in a monotonous loop. Whatever music was on the radio, I didn't want to hear, so I shut it off. Swaddled in the sweet silence of my car, I suddenly got this overwhelming feeling that someone was sitting in the passenger seat next to me. The sensation was *so* strong, *so* potent that I was actually afraid to turn my head and look. I stayed facing forward and focused on the road stretching out ahead of me. But tears spilled out of my eyes as I felt this cocoon enwrap me, like I was physically being enveloped by a cloud of... *support? Love?* The sensation was utterly disorienting. I was crying but I was also so very deeply happy somehow. There was a kind of euphoria to being held this way. It felt like what I imagine floating in space at zero gravity might be like. The feeling was so overpowering I had to force myself to remember that I was driving a two-ton vehicle at seventy miles an hour. I gripped the steering wheel to ground myself, as I was suddenly made aware of the speed of the car. That presence was still there, it was sitting right next to me. I was dangling in this otherworldly space, driving on the freeway with an invisible passenger. *How is this happening?* I let my eyes dart to my right, entirely expecting to see my father sitting there. But I didn't see his physical body there. What I saw was something I can only describe as a sense of density to the air, a fullness to the empty seat that told me *This is blessed. Let this be your salvation.*

When I walked in my front door later that afternoon, I realized that I had been hiding in my own home. Dodging my father in the dining room. Evading him in the kitchen. *What if I just stopped sidestepping and stood still?* I walked into the center of my living room and just stood there. I exhaled an enormous deep breath. I let my muscles settle, relaxed into my bones, felt my feet on the floor. I let the soft bubble of my soul come to the surface and absorb what was around me. I embraced it all and my knees buckled.

"Hi," I whispered. "I miss you."

Maybe you're thinking that I was imagining all of this. That those were just the musings of a lonely and bruised being. And maybe you're right. But maybe you aren't.

I began to really embrace how thin the veil is in between worlds. Between consciousness and the unconscious. This life and the last. This life and the next. I let any of my residual fear and anxiety surrounding those ideas dissolve into a warm curiosity, a calm acceptance of a much bigger picture which, if I really thought about it, I had always been driven by since as far back as I could remember. I surrendered to the utter uncertainty that lay ahead of me. And I let my broken heart be just a little more broken, releasing the stifling grip I'd been keeping on it in the hopes I would be able to save myself from any more grief. And this simple, un-pinpoint-able shift at once freed me and buoyed me to safety. I finally let my end be my beginning.

chapter
FOURTEEN

The ways I have changed are immeasurable. Some indistinguishable, others as though I have tattooed my forehead or grown a third arm.

I don't get scared on subways at night, for example. I don't fear flying in airplanes or terrorist attacks in shopping malls. These fears are absurd to me. Not to sound trite but, truly, in a nutshell: If it's my time, it's my time. And why imagine something awful that has some small percentage of happening when it only devours the very finite and invaluable time we have here in the present? I don't fear TV producers or network executives or get intimidated by someone smarter, taller, prettier, more talented, skinnier, or wealthier than me. These things are simply a waste of time. What I really fear? Not doing something meaningful with my life every single day. And the thought of growing old without love can send me into a panic far more intense than how my ass may look in a particular pair of jeans. I have, in a word, grown up.

None of these things are extraordinary. And all of these things are extraordinary.

I think about nourishing myself and planting roots in fertile ground rather than dried-out soil. I listen more and I (try to) judge people less. I'm empathic on a level I can't articulate and sometimes that feels like too much, but it also allows my heart to be full. I'm turned on by kindness and expression and authenticity. Genuineness makes me *high*. I have little patience for cruelty or flagrant disregard for another human being, for one thing is certain: we will all die one day, and this destiny we all unequivocally share bonds us. And if that does not make us equals, our hearts and our souls surely do.

I've learned that while the ego screams, intuition whispers. And whispers can be delicious. I have fallen in love and loved someone and learned the difference between the two. I have come to the conclusion that *who* is in my life is far more important than *what*. And I have learned that I shape my life, that *I* am responsible for following my dreams.

I've learned that faith doesn't come when things are peachy keen. Faith is usually birthed when you feel so broken that you don't know how you will put another foot forward. I've learned that in those moments it can feel like nothing will ever change. But the truth is things are changing all of the time. Every second, every moment, we are evolving.

I've missed my father and become closer to my mother. I've followed the footprints of those who have walked before me, and then forged my own path. I have wondered and wandered, thought I was losing my mind. I've felt so raw I was certain that everyone could see the outline of my heart inside my chest. And I've learned that when we let our hearts break like that, we discover our affinity to all other human beings. We inch toward intimacy, inch our way into one another's hearts.

I've learned to sit with the pain and hang on through the darkness. To hang on until the very last moment when a tiny sliver of light always appears at the end of the tunnel. Sometimes it's so slight that it could almost be mistaken for a mirage, the hallucination of a soul desperate for saving. But slowly that flickering of hope becomes a constant glow, and the body moves toward it tentatively, putting one heavy-soled foot in front of the other until you reach up to hold the rays of light between your fingers.

I've seen how our darkest moments can truly bring the greatest of gifts.

———

I had one more visitation dream with my dad that I remember as vividly as I do the first. It began without much consequence. I got into bed one night, closed my eyes, and what felt like almost immediately, I went to sleep.

My eyes flutter open and I see shimmering light and warm colors. Things come into focus and I find that I'm strolling on the sidewalk of a charming suburban street. The street is lined with happy houses and green lawns, saturated in pleasant sunshine and a soft breeze. As I stroll, I come across a girl walking a horse. *I know this horse! I've taken care of this horse before.* I go to pet him and say hello and he rears up wildly, whinnying and grunting. The girl is nonplussed as she's pulled left and right by his strength.

I hear my voice say, "Is it because the horse doesn't like me?" The girl grins at me in this confusing way, like maybe that was a silly question. Then the horse really goes berserk and gets loose. And now there are other horses, a dozen maybe, galloping wild on the streets of this lovely neighborhood. It is disorderly and odd but not dangerous. Just carefree chaos.

Then suddenly amid this sunny mayhem, Dad is here. He's sick but has a clarity about him and he's quite coherent. We embrace tightly, warmly, and this soothes me beyond words. I'm aware that somehow this hug tells him everything about my life now; it transmits how I am and who I am. I go to speak but my mouth doesn't move, and I hear my voice in that pure, distilled vibration say, "Dad, I will miss you so much."

I face him head on, look directly into his soul, and my whole being says, "I'm so sad that you won't be here for so many things in my life. I am who I am because of you." The words ripple through me and are absorbed right into him. Then my tone shifts ever so slightly. "You're sick, Dad. And you aren't going to make it."

I'm expecting resistance. I am braced for his rebuttal but am surprised to find that he doesn't argue. And then right in this moment, Dad looks at me and shows me his last days on earth. They play out right before my eyes instantaneously, all of his rage at the world and at me. As well as my final moment with him before he died, when I looked at his clenched fists and listened to his labored breathing and I whispered into his ear to "be free" and "picture bright blue skies and just float to peace." All of this travels through me in an instant. Then with a final acknowledgement and acceptance, as if he has been the architect of this whole visit, Dad looks directly in my eyes and he nods.

And for the first time, we truly see each other.

He takes my hand in his and places both of them over my heart.

He hugs me deeply.

I feel his love for me and his understanding and his pride.

And I know he is saying goodbye.

I woke up in my bed and I was still in the hug, smiling. The physical sensation was all through my body and I felt warm. The realization poured over me that I had a deeper relationship with my father now that he was gone than I ever did when he was alive.

This is not the end.

It is a beginning.

Nothing is irreparable.

It's never too late.

There is always hope.

Always, there is hope.

So maybe the heart hammered in grief unleashes our angelic light. And although this life is not always pretty, sometimes it is gorgeous. Gorgeous and terrifying, delicate and violent, familiar and strange, enormous and very, very small. Sometimes it is perverse, and most of us most of the time don't have a clue what we are doing. But it is glorious, this life. And when we are grateful and paying attention, we can live this life as we are meant to— with open eyes and an open heart.

Epilogue

Dear Dad,

I wonder what you're thinking right now.

"Why did I let her ride horses around and make movies in the basement when she was eight? I knew I should have made her go to business school."

Ha! Just kidding... sort of.

Well, look, we have a lot of ground to cover so I guess I should just get started.

First of all, a question: How deliriously was your head spinning when I actually got married? *Right*? Never expected that one, I'm sure. I asked Mom what she thought you would say about Charlie and me getting married *after* I had the baby. After a long pause she said, "OH, I'M PRETTY SURE YOUR DAD WOULD JUST BE HAPPY YOU'RE GETTING MARRIED AT ALL!" Ha. And how crazy is it that he's a Jets fan? You realize the extent of my interest in and knowledge of football has only been *your* love of the Jets. So when Charlie said he was a Jets fan, I naturally assumed that everybody loves the Jets, that they must be a fan favorite of the entire football community. I mean, wow was I wrong about that. I'm learning just how much you and Charlie would have to commiserate about in that regard.

Anyway, you'd like Charlie. He's one you could kick back and have a beer with but still be able to talk business to. He'd impress you, Dad, but he's not pompous. You guys are alike in that way, not needing to impress anyone, gauging people's validity based on their ability to refrain from telling you everything they have. I bet I'd have to tear you two apart at the holidays. And forget about at horse shows.

And Scarlett. People always say she has your nose, especially when she was a baby. Genes are funny like that, aren't they? And oh Dad, she is a riot. She's never played with dolls, she likes math and plays the electric guitar and wears goggles and weird outfits, and she's always building things. And she plays soccer like a total baller. She has a very serious mind of her own and an independent spirit. She's a negotiator and a thinker, also has legendary emotional swings. Sound familiar? I'm certain that her teenage years will prove to be penance for my own. By the way, did I ever apologize for, like, most of the '80s? If not, sorry for that. Yeah, parenting really teaches you what you never thought you didn't know, if you know what I mean, and I'm sure you do. Anyway, you would absolutely adore her. I'm always telling her that too. I wish you could be here with us to watch her grow up. You know, Mom went to see this psychic the other day who said that you held Scarlett before she crossed over to us here. That you held her in your arms and hugged her. I burst into tears when she told me because it didn't surprise me in the least. I always felt like you two knew one another somehow. I mean, she has the sixth sense, obviously. When I got that phone call that things had fallen through with the initial funding for the film—yes, *this* film, the film about you—and I started crying in the kitchen? She was so little and had no idea what I was crying about. But out of the blue, without knowing what it was, never having seen it before, she rummaged through the kitchen drawer and found your old watch. I nearly fell over. She just held it out to me with a smile. She blows my mind regularly. She also knew that Charlie's dad passed away before we did. No joke. She was just four years old. It was July, and I was about to take her to summer camp for the day when she informed me she had to pack her suitcase to go to "BB and Billy's." I thought she was just confused; we had a trip planned for August to go visit them. So I told her that we weren't leaving for a month, that she had the timing mixed up. She became irritated with me and kept saying, "No! We are going tomorrow. It's tomorrow. I have to pack my bag!" So I figured, whatever, let her have her purple hippo knapsack on wheels packed for five weeks, who cares? As soon as I dropped her off at summer camp, Charlie called and said his dad was in an ambulance on the way to the hospital and they had to decide whether to keep him alive on machines. Within minutes of turning off the machines, he passed. And guess when we flew to New Jersey? The next day. When she got home from camp and I told her that we had to fly to see BB tomorrow, she looked at me like I was a real dummy. "I know, I already told you that!" she said. She's a force, but she has such a sensitive soul. I'm guessing you already know that. She's a real badass, Dad. Forgive the profanity, but she really is.

And you know who else, it turns out, is also pretty much a badass? Mom. *YEAH, I know!* I mean yes, she is still loopy and I'm fairly certain she should not be operating a motor vehicle after four p.m., but she is literally a unicorn. She's an eighty-year-old with the energy and the spirit of a teenager, always the life of the party. She has friends twenty years her junior that can't keep up with her. Both of her cancers and all of her surgeries and she's back playing golf several times a week and "blogging" about the movies she sees with the ladies. Yes, she has a blog. Full transparency, she still leaves me voicemails that start with, "Honey, it's Mom. ARE YOU THERE? PICK UP!" but for the most part she has adapted quite nicely to the digital world. Still doesn't know how to cook, however. Chicken parm like rubber, like it's been in the oven for a decade.

Oh, before I forget—I'm not exactly sure how much you had to do with this, but thanks for stopping that car accident in North Carolina after Mom's second surgery. I was so stressed out and scattered trying to get to Nikki's to pick up Scarlett, my mind was I-don't-know-where. But I know that car was about to hit me and it would have 100 percent been my fault and I was driving way too fast and I didn't even see the stop sign. Moments like that are the dictionary definition of "your life flashing before you." That excruciating extended honking of the horn. The skid marks I left on the road, and the slow-motion sound and whipping wind of the car blowing by me. I just sat there spun around in the middle of the road in the middle of nowhere. I mean, talk about pulling a Hail Mary. If it wasn't you, it was definitely one of the team up there, so please extend my gratitude. That goes for all of your nudges and messages; I hear them and I'm grateful. The encouragement and reassurance have been like a lifeboat at times.

Speaking of, how's it all going for you up and out there? Are you bored with all of the metaphysical closure and understanding and greater enlightenment you must have now? Feel free to impart any and all secrets to me, I'm a much better listener now. And while I definitely don't know all of the answers, I do know that I'm really fortunate. You taught me how to be a good person, Dad. And I don't know if I ever told you that exactly. So thanks.

Well, I guess I just wanted you to know that I'm thinking of you. I want you to know that it's not only when I feel alone and terrified and incapable of taking care of myself that I think of you and wish you could hug me and make it all better. It's for the good stuff too. I wish you were here now for all of this. But I know how much of a hand you've had in it. Maybe it's all happening as a psychic domino effect and the worst things to happen have led me on this labyrinthine journey to the happiest of endings. If that's the case, it kind of seems like a sick joke on behalf of the Universe. But I guess that's part of the whole ball of wax, so to speak. Whole nine yards? Kit and caboodle? You get my point.

I'll keep this short, because I'm already feeling like I'm gonna start crying and then it'll be like I'm the kid again looking for comfort, which wasn't my intention in writing to you. But I guess we always are, aren't we? We're always our parents' children, no matter what age, I suppose? I understand that so fiercely now.

I love you so much, Dad. And I miss you almost all of the time, which totally throws me. But it's weird, because I always know you're here. Just when I need you. There's this chair I sit in at my dining room table, the chair I'm sitting in right now, and it's like a portal. A gateway to this in-between place, where you and I are on the same level, in the same space, the same place. And I get you, and you get me. And it's like we're hanging out. I feel that right now.

I hope you read this and you hear Ella and Louis crooning in the background, and it's like a warm summer night and you're humming to yourself with your feet up on the ottoman in your slippers, tapping your foot and doing a crossword puzzle.

And I'm sitting right next to you.

XOXO

Wheez

Acknowledgments

It's impossible to know where to start with these.

My immense gratitude to:

Susan Mears: Thank you for your belief in me and for representing this book with grace and authenticity.

Amy Glaser: You are an editor extraordinaire. Your passion for this book was invaluable. Thank you for your articulate and spot-on notes and insights, for withstanding my countless emails, questions, and revisions, and reminding us both to "Hang in There" (insert cat poster here).

All of the artists and musicians on my writing soundtrack: I wrote this book with the constant accompaniment of your music. Thank you for your inspiration. (If readers are interested in hearing it, I have a Spotify playlist "Wake Me When You Leave.")

Teresa Symes: Your guidance, connection, and consistency have kept me afloat through troubled waters for many years now. Thank you for keeping me on track. And Steve Dennis: Your early support, input, and intuition on this book were invaluable.

The Sweet Dreams Team/The Magic, aka Nancy Lainer and Eileen McHale: You guys believed in the magic of this project from the beginning as a play, and your dedication and smarts gave this story its first legs. I love you both dearly and cherish our friendship deeply. #yourewelcome.

All of the friends and colleagues who provided input and support on the play version of this early on, especially Aaron McPherson, Maria Maggenti, Jeffrey Tambor, Nell Scovell, and April Webster.

All of the Creative Dreamers: Your artistry and imaginations have collectively supported me creatively, unconsciously, and at times physically. Especially Kim Gillingham, Doug Barber, Ken Barnett, Sandra Oh, Rosemarie DeWitt, Missy Yager, Ronit Kirchman, Jennifer Grey, Meta Golding, Derek Simonds.

The real Milo, the real Martin, and the real Cooper: I hope you all read this and feel what forces for good you've been in my life. I am grateful for the lessons and I love you all. You're welcome in my dreams anytime.

Cerina Vincent, my angel, soul sister, and fellow Aquarian warrior: Your intuition, creative support, friendship, and love have buoyed me to sanity. And Annika Marks: Your friendship, creative support, and fierce loyalty have carried me.

Shawn: I hope I did you justice and helped people remember your name, Smiley. And Matt O.: Thank you for letting me use your beautiful lyrics.

Debbie Grant: Thank you for your patience and guidance. They saved me more times than I can count.

Danielle, who was in the trenches with me while on her own beaten path: Our phone calls picked me up off the cold floor I was usually lying on. I'm sorry the pain of that period of time tore us apart. I will always cherish the depth and length of our friendship, Schmoopie.

Leo, my Aquarian comrade: Thank you for helping me express through the darkness and for holding me when I cried. A lot.

Melanie, Camilla, and Afton Place: Thank you for the hijinks and the hugs. (And thank you for helping me pack the night before I went home, Melanie. I always remember that … how does one pack for such a trip?) And Mike S. for the countless hangs and drinks and adventures.

Natalie, Meredith, and Jen B.: For the tarot, the walks, and the talks that comforted me immensely.

Book Club: Maria, Gina, Michelle, Leslie, Alexa, Katy, and Cory (and Dana M., you're an honorary member): Thank you for supporting me and being my guinea pigs with this book. You ladies fill my heart.

Sarah Taylor: Our Tuesday nights helped my revisions immeasurably. Thank you for reminding me to let "Jesus take the wheel," even when he doesn't seem like a very good driver.

Charlie: I hope you read this and understand the me that was before we met. Thank you for the patience and support. I love you. Maybe this will be the year for the Jets.

Scarlett: Thank you for not complaining at all about me having to work on the weekends through the pandemic to make the deadline for this book (insert head exploding here). I love you beyond words. I hope when you are allowed to read this it helps you know who Grandpa Jack was. I also hope it shows you how important it is to work hard and follow your passions.

Mom, Pam, and Marc: Your wackiness and instability have obviously contributed much to the content of this book. Just kidding, guys! Just checking to see if you are actually reading this. I love you all. Thank you for letting me share my experience of us.

And finally, to my dad, Jack Donovan: Thank you for providing me with my soul's purpose. I hope this sings to you and makes you proud.

Author's Note

These acknowledgments would be incomplete if I didn't also acknowledge doing the revisions on this book during a pandemic and the accompanying lockdowns, coupled with the international protests against brutal racial violence in the United States. The world was experiencing the death of life as we all once knew it. And feeling the collective grief for the loss of lives and livelihoods while I was holed up writing this book about grief was surreal to say the least. This time period engendered an uprising, a revolution of the minds and spirits of so many. And at the same time, I felt a kind of retreat and a return to simplicity—a slower-paced, more authentic, and less bloated daily life. I thought a lot about our discomfort as a culture with talking about grief and the parallels with our discomfort with talking about race. And I thought about how destructive silence can be on both fronts. My hope is that when this book comes out, we are all tending to one another and to the collective aspiration for a better world.

Photo Section

With Dad when I was one year old, 1972.

With Drew, 1975.

Rita, Drew, and me when I was 8, 1979.

At the pony club competition in 1984.

Competing at the spring horse trials in the junior
novice category in 1985. Photo credit: Mary Phelps.

Competing at the spring horse trials in the junior
novice category in 1985. Photo credit: Mary Phelps.

Self-portrait, 1986.

Me, Rita, Mom, Dad, and Drew, 1992.

With Drew, 1993.

Zulie when she was a puppy, 1995.

Zulie in the house I was living in when Shawn came to visit.

Dad's retirement dinner in New York
City, 1998. Drew, Dad, me, and Rita.

Mom and Dad on their anniversary, 1998.

After my ER visit to treat a scratched
cornea on the day of Dad's funeral, 2004.

Scattering Dad's ashes with Mom, 2004.

A plaque dedicating the pavillion at the
Carolina Horse Park in my dad's memory, 2004.

Me, Drew, and Rita, 1974.

My first grade school picture.

Photo credit: Leo Canneto.

My friend Leo Canneto took these photos of me
for the Art Project. Yes, that is me having a picnic in the
middle of Sunset Boulevard. Photo credit: Leo Canneto.

Photo credit: Leo Canneto.

The dollar bill that said "Sapphire" that I received
in change when I went to see *Big Fish*, 2004.